FAMILY MATTERS
✓

BARBECUE HINTS AND TIPS

FAMILY MATTERS ✓

BARBECUE HINTS AND TIPS

BRIDGET JONES

WARD LOCK

First published in 1990 by Ward Lock
Artillery House, Artillery Row, London SW1P 1RT, England
A Cassell imprint

British Library Cataloguing in Publication Data
Jones, Bridget
  Barbecue Hints and Tips.
  1. Food: Barbecue dishes – Recipes
  I. Title   II. Series
  641.7'6

  ISBN 0-7063-6893-2

Printed and bound in Great Britain by Collins

Thanks are due to Thermos Limited
for information on, and loan of a gas
barbecue

Special Note:

All Microwave timings are intended as a guide when cooking in a 650
watt oven.

All recipes serve 4 unless otherwise stated.

USING THIS BOOK

Barbecue Hints and Tips is written for the first-time barbecue cook as well as for anyone who is hoping to extend their repertoire of al fresco grilling beyond preparing sausages and burgers. In the opening pages, *Buying a Barbecue* provides a comprehensive guide to the wide range of barbecues, from a simple grill to a sophisticated gas-powered appliance. Read through this section if you are thinking of buying your first barbecue or if you want to move on to bigger and better equipment.

Before you rush outdoors to cook, check the details in *Lighting Up*. So many people have problems getting the barbecue going that I have included a short section explaining how to light up safely and successfully, and when to begin cooking.

Once your barbecue is good and hot you can use it for cooking all sorts of food. The A–Z guide lists a variety of savoury and sweet foods to barbecue, with basic instructions and timings as well as recipe ideas. In this section you will also find information on the wide range of barbecue accessories that are available; on planning a barbecue party; organizing the menu; herbs, spices and seasonings; marinades; side dishes, salads and cool drinks.

With plenty of hints and tips, there is all the information to ensure that every barbecue is a roaring success. Use the recipe index at the back of the book to look up specific recipes.

BUYING A BARBECUE

Have a good look around the hardware shops, garden
centres, larger supermarkets, cook's shops and depart-
ment stores to discover an amazing array of barbecues
and accessories, from disposable charcoal grills to
electric barbecues built into smart patio trolleys.
Between these extremes, there is a good choice of
inexpensive barbecues (some portable), moderately
priced models and sturdy products that will give many
years' service. You can pay anything from a few pounds
to a few hundred pounds.

To discuss all the features of every type would fill
the book; however, consider these general features:

★ **MATERIAL** The better the quality of material used to
make the barbecue, the longer it will last. Light, thin,
sheet metal models will not wear as well as cast iron
barbecues.

★ **STABILITY** Whether it is portable or fixed on a large
stand, the barbecue must be stable when it is set up
on a level surface.

★ **ADEQUATE FIREBOWL** There must be room to burn
enough charcoal for the cooking area. Look at the
depth of the firebowl as well as its width. Make sure
that it is deep enough to hold a reasonable volume of
hot coals safely.

★ ***COOKING HEIGHTS*** Check that the cooking rack is a sensible distance above the charcoal to avoid burning food. Look for variable cooking height – even small barbecues allow for the cooking rack to be slotted into two or three positions.

★ ***SAFE MANUFACTURE*** Check that the seams and any metal joints are fairly sturdy and that there are no rough edges on the outside of the barbecue. When buying a gas or electric barbecue, look for information on whether the product meets the requirements set by British Standards.

DISPOSABLE BARBECUES

Small foil barbecues containing self-lighting charcoal. They are designed to light in 10 minutes and to burn for up to 2 hours. The cooking area is large enough for about four chops or chicken portions, or for eight sausages. Good for picnics or camping, pack the number required to cook the quantity of food. Available in supermarkets.

PORTABLE BARBECUES

The simplest portable barbecue is just one step up from the disposable type: a small metal container to hold the charcoal, with raised sides into which the cooking grill may be slotted at two levels. The top of the metal may be notched to hold up to five skewers. No handle but this type is small enough to put in a plastic bag to take on a picnic.

The true 'portable' barbecue is one that folds up neatly with a handle for carrying it. An oblong barbecue is typical of this type, with the firebowl forming the carrying case when closed. The lid of the case is hinged to provide a wind shield during cooking. The legs may be very short or detachable: in some models the legs are used as the handle when packed.

At least one major manufacturer produces a small kettle barbecue on short detachable legs, ideal for taking on picnics or for home cooking. Having a lid, this type may be used for cooking joints as well as smaller items of food.

Some of the larger barbecues come with separate carrying cases. If you want a model to pack easily, make sure of this before you buy.

CAST IRON TABLE-TOP BARBECUES

Very simple, cast iron firebowl with a stainless steel cooking rack that sits at one level on top of the firebowl. Small and basic, this type of barbecue is useful for foods that cook quickly and successfully near the coals: small cuts of meat and boneless poultry, fish, quick-cooking vegetables, bananas and so on. It is important to avoid overfilling the firebowl and to have the charcoal thoroughly heated before cooking. Having only one cooking height, near the coals, this type of barbecue is limiting. However, it is stable and high quality.

HIBACHI GRILLS

Made from cast iron or pressed steel these small, inexpensive barbecues stand up to hard wear.

The heavy oblong firebowl has wooden handles and it stands on two short feet. The bowl has vents in the base and a slightly raised rack on which to burn the charcoal. Cooking racks with wooden handles slot into support grids fixed to the back of the firebowl. The grids provide three or four cooking levels. Available in two sizes, the larger one having three or four small, square cooking racks.

Inexpensive, uncomplicated and sturdy given that it is placed on a good, stable, heatproof surface: a good buy.

ROUND METAL BARBECUES

Free-standing, round barbecues with a firebowl and wind shield which incorporates slots for the cooking rack to be positioned at different heights. Quality varies: from very cheap, lightweight sheet metal models to heavy-gauge steel, well-finished examples.

This type of barbecue is supported on three legs: check that they do not wobble feebly when in place. Some have a small shelf underneath and/or a fixed canopy with a chimney. This chimneyed canopy is intended to create a draught and to direct the cooking smoke upwards. The cheaper models are good first-time barbecues but the very thin metal ones do not withstand a lot of wear.

Look out for cast iron barbecues of this type if you want to spend more. A practical feature is a rotating cooking rack allowing for easy removal, or turning, of food cooked at the back of the barbecue.

HORIZONTAL OR VERTICAL COOKING BARBECUES

Some oblong barbecues may be used in a horizontal or vertical position. A rack encloses the hot coals in the firebowl which may be tilted through 90° so that it locks in a vertical position. This can then be used only for spit-roasting; the fat from the spit-roasted food is caught in a drip tray.

Another type of barbecue designed for vertical cooking has a high windshield which curves into a narrow canopy at the back. A double cooking rack enclosing the food slots into the top of the canopy and into a drip tray at the front of the barbecue. The fat collects in the drip tray, although the handle of the cooking rack does get greasy. The disadvantage of using an enclosed cooking rack is that if foods of different thicknesses are placed in the rack, the thin ones slip down. Irregular-shaped pieces of food cannot be cooked in this way; similarly foods that squash easily may not be successfully enclosed in the rack.

So, if you are thinking of buying this type of model, make sure that the barbecue can cook food horizontally as well as vertically.

KETTLE BARBECUES

This type has a domed firebowl with some form of ash collection and removal system, and vents. A domed lid, with vents, may be kept on during cooking or rested on the back of the barbecue to act as a windshield.

The cooking rack fits inside the firebowl at different heights to allow for fast or slow cooking. Various racks are available for holding joints of meat, vegetables, kebabs, steaks or chops.

Joints and whole birds may be cooked in the closed barbecue, speeding up cooking. The heat from the coals

is reflected off the lid and the inside of the barbecue acts as an oven.

TROLLEY BARBECUES

They vary in size but tend to be larger and more sophisticated, also more expensive.

This term may be applied to a wide range of models that have two wheels. Some of the small round barbecues and kettle barbecues also have wheels. Here I am using the term to distinguish the large, oblong barbecues.

The simplest model usually allows for accessories to be fitted to one side of the cooking area, for example wooden or metal stands and utensil racks. The most sophisticated has two firebowls and cooking racks, stands for bottles, a shelf underneath, a board to the side and space for hanging utensils.

Some models have a shallow warming oven underneath the firebowl – useful for heating pitta bread or garlic bread, or for keeping batches of barbecued food

hot if you are cooking for a crowd and want to serve lots of food at once.

Some barbecues have warming racks that stand above and to the back of the cooking area.

BRICK BARBECUES

This may be a permanent feature of the patio, with the bricks or concrete blocks cemented in place, or the bricks can be stacked without cement for dismantling, if wished, at a later date.

Walls should be constructed at the back and sides of the barbecue. Kits including an ash plate, fire rack and cooking rack may be purchased. These also include metal clips to be fixed into the brickwork at different levels above the fire rack. However the different racks may be purchased separately or a large paving slab may be used instead of the ash plate.

Construct the brick walls so that the ash tray or paving slab fits securely into the sides and back. The fire rack should stand securely on top of the ash tray and should be removable for easy disposal of the ash. Remember to include supports for the cooking rack – either turn four bricks around so that they jut out into the middle of the barbecue (good if you are not cementing them in place) or build in small metal plates or clips.

As well as kits for building a charcoal barbecue, gas barbecues are available in the form of build-in kits.

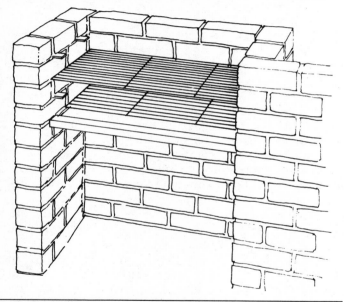

GAS BARBECUES

Large gas barbecues are at the top end of the market. However, the smaller models are comparable, price-wise, with the middle-of-the-range charcoal barbecues.

Instead of using charcoal, this type of barbecue burns gas supplied from a canister. The gas is fed to jets which burn under the cooking rack. The burning jets may be covered with lava rock or with rows of 'V' shaped metal strips. The food is cooked on a rack over the heated rock or metal strips, either on the open barbecue or with the lid closed.

Individual manufacturers provide instructions for lighting and heating the barbecue before cooking. Gas barbecues heat up far more quickly than charcoal. The barbecue usually has more than one burner and both are used initially until the surface is hot enough for cooking. Adjustable controls allow for the heat to be raised or lowered during cooking.

Barbecued food takes its flavour from the juices that drip on to the hot surface creating cooking 'smoke' which rises. Therefore, in theory, gas barbecues should give the food a similar flavour to charcoal barbecues that are heated correctly before cooking. For the best flavour, keep the lid on a gas barbecue during cooking. As with any barbecuing, foods that take slightly longer to cook have a better flavour. Hickory chips, or other scented wood products used for smoking food, may be wrapped in pierced foil or placed on a foil tray and put on top of the heat source to flavour the food during cooking.

The advantage of gas barbecues is that they are quick and easy to light, clean and convenient. Built on trolleys they are easy to move from place to place. If the weather takes a turn for the worse, the lid on a gas barbecue may be closed and the food will continue to cook. Because this type of barbecue does not create a lot of smoke in the initial stages, it is ideal for using under a car port or in a well-ventilated open garage. Always remember to observe common sense safety rules and use the barbecue in a safe, well-ventilated place.

As well as the cost of the barbecue, the other initial financial outlay is for the cylinder of gas; however, the cost of re-charging the gas cylinder is fairly small. Essentially, a gas barbecue is no more expensive to run than a charcoal barbecue – if anything it may be cheaper.

Features on gas barbecues include shelves to the side of and under the cooking area, a warming rack, rotisserie facility and a viewing window in some barbecue lids. The most sophisticated models also include a small gas ring for heating sauces and so on.

When buying a gas barbecue do check up on safety standards; some are tested and meet the requirements of the relevant British Standard. The key point to remember when lighting a gas barbecue is that the lid must be kept open until the appliance is properly lit. Never turn the gas supply on with the lid closed.

ELECTRIC BARBECUES

This type of barbecue has an electric element with lava rock, or chips of it, on top. The element is used to heat the rock and the food is cooked on a rack above. Obviously, an electric barbecue must be sited near a power point or a safe extension lead be used to connect the barbecue to the power supply. Electric barbecues are of questionable value as outdoor appliances.

ROTISSERIES

All but the smallest barbecues and hibachi grills have the facility for using a battery-operated rotisserie. Useful for cooking whole birds such as chicken or duck, joints of meat or kebabs (depending on individual design).

LIGHTING UP

If you have a gas barbecue, this stage will be problem free!

Remove the cooking rack so that the fire may be mounded up for lighting. The barbecue can be laid with paper and fine wood kindling, then the charcoal or briquettes placed on top. If you do use wood to start the fire, the pieces must be very fine, otherwise the charcoal may be burnt out before the wood, resulting in unwanted smoke.

> **Never** *use petrol or paraffin to light a barbecue and never pour methylated spirits on to burning charcoal or on to a barbecue.*

Instead of wood, try using fire lighters or barbecue lighters. Break off two or three pieces of lighter and place them in between the pieces of charcoal, mounding the charcoal around each piece but not covering it completely.

Barbecue lighting sachets and pastes are available and they should be put between the pieces of charcoal, following the manufacturer's instructions.

Barbecue lighting fuel should be used according to the manufacturer's instructions. It is usually squirted over the charcoal, then allowed to soak in before the barbecue is lit.

Alternatively, self-lighting charcoal may be purchased.

The whole bag of charcoal is placed in the firebowl and ignited. The charcoal inside the bag is impregnated with lighting material.

Although methylated spirits must never be poured on to a barbecue which is lit, it can be added to some charcoal placed in a polythene bag. Put about a dozen pieces of charcoal or briquettes in a polythene bag. Pour a little methylated spirits over the charcoal in the bag, then twist the end of the bag closed, shake up the charcoal and set it aside to soak up the spirits for about 15 minutes. Replace the lid on the bottle of spirits and put it away. When laying the barbecue, tip the charcoal from the polythene bag on top of a few pieces of charcoal and surround with more charcoal. Discard the polythene bag in a rubbish bin, away from the barbecue. The charcoal impregnated with spirits will light easily. **Never use methylated spirits in any other way to light a barbecue**.

Once the barbecue is laid, use long matches to light it and leave it to burn until all the charcoal is well lit. Once all the charcoal is burning (after about 20 minutes) it should be spread out and left to burn until it has turned white and all the flames have subsided. This is when the fuel is at its hottest and ready for cooking.

If you begin to cook food over charcoal that is still flaming or only partly burning, strong, unpleasant smoke rises and the food will flare up quite easily. Be patient – allow at least 30 minutes for the charcoal to get hot enough for cooking. Most types of charcoal will take about 40 minutes, depending on the amount used. Obviously, the larger the barbecue, the longer it takes to burn through.

> **Golden rule:** *wait until the charcoal burns to an even, hot-ash grey colour before cooking.*

★ **TOPPING UP** If you are cooking a lot of food, you may have to top up the barbecue with extra fuel. Pile some charcoal or briquettes to one side of the barbecue, where they will get hot without burning. When the barbecue needs topping up just shovel them on and they will burn quickly. If you are adding cold fuel, shovel in small amounts at a time and to one side, or use fire tongs to put extra charcoal around the outside of the fire.

★ **LIGHTING A GAS BARBECUE** Follow the manufacturer's instructions. Open the lid before turning the gas supply on and leave the lid open until the barbecue is lit. The barbecue is usually lit by turning one gas source to high and pressing an ignition button. Once lit, the lid should be shut and the barbecue preheated for the recommended time – about 5 minutes. The controls offer different heat settings and these should be selected according to the food. The heat settings are used instead of altering the distance between the food and charcoal on a conventional barbecue.

★ **BURNING OUT** When you have finished cooking, leave the charcoal to burn out if it has not already done so.

A

APPLES

Both cooking and eating apples may be barbecued. Eating apples are easiest.

Caramelized Apples

Quarter and core eating apples, then dip the pieces in lemon juice and coat the cut sides with caster sugar. Thread on to metal skewers and cook for 2–3 minutes on each side, until the sugar has turned to caramel.

Baked Apples

Core small cooking apples (one per person) and score their skin around the middle. Place an apple on a piece of buttered foil. Fill the hole left by the core with soft brown sugar, adding a good pinch of ground cinnamon. Top with a knob of butter and close the foil around the apple. When all the apples are packed cook them on the barbecue rack for 30–40 minutes, turning the parcels over halfway through, until the apples are soft. Barbecue the apples when you finish cooking the savoury food, then they will be ready to serve when everyone has eaten the main course.

★ **APPLE SAUCE** Cook over the hob as an accompaniment to barbecued food. Peel, core and slice 450 g/1 lb cooking apples, then cook them to a pulp with a strip of lemon peel and 50 g/2 oz sugar. Beat in a good knob of butter. Serve with pork, gammon, sausages or duck.

▶ Wrap chunks of eating apple in halved rindless bacon rashers, thread on to skewers and barbecue until crisp (see Prunes, page 98). Good for starters!

AUBERGINES

Aubergine Rolls

Trim large aubergines and cut a fine slice of skin lengthways off each one; discard this. Cut the aubergines lengthways into 5-mm/ ¼-in thick slices, discarding the remaining fine slice of skin. Layer the slices in a colander, sprinkling with salt, and leave for 30 minutes. Rinse and drain, then blanch the slices in boiling water for 2 minutes. Drain and lay on absorbent kitchen paper to dry and cool.

Soften a 150-g/5-oz packet of cream cheese with herbs and garlic (for example Boursin), then mix

in 50 g/2 oz fresh breadcrumbs.
Place a small sausage shape of this
mixture at one end of each aubergine slice. Roll up, coat lightly in
flour and thread on to two long
skewers. The rolls may be covered
and chilled overnight if wished:
they are easier to handle if chilled
for at least 30 minutes.

Brush the rolls with olive oil
and cook fairly near the coals for
10–12 minutes, turning once or
twice, until browned on both sides.
Serve as a starter (enough for
four) with Tomato Sauce (page
115) or Basil Tomato Concassé
(page 116). Also a good vegetarian
main course for two or three.

Skewered Aubergines

Trim the ends off medium aubergines, cut lengthways into quarters,
then across into large chunks. One
medium aubergine will serve two.
Place the chunks in a colander,
sprinkle with salt and leave over a
bowl for 30 minutes. Rinse and
drain well. Thread the chunks on
to long metal skewers, brush
generously with olive oil and
sprinkle with just a little dried
oregano. Chopped fresh oregano
may be used more generously
than the dried herb. Cook at a
medium height over the coals for
about 10 minutes, turning once or
twice, until browned and tender.
Good with lamb or pork.

AVOCADOS

Roasted halved avocados taste terrific! Halve a ripe avocado, remove the stone and brush the cut side with a little oil. Sprinkle with just a hint of dried sage and some freshly grated nutmeg. Place cut side down on the cooking rack, fairly near the coals, and leave for about 2–3 minutes, until browned. Use a slice to turn the avocados over, then cook, skin side down, for 2–3 minutes. Serve hot, with lemon or lime wedges, or soured cream with chives, and crusty bread.

Try other seasonings instead of sage and nutmeg: grated lemon or lime rind and a little juice; a little chopped fresh coriander; rub with a cut clove of garlic before brushing with oil, then top with shredded fresh basil before serving.

Avocado and Bacon Kebabs

Halve a firm, ripe avocado. Remove the stone and quarter lengthways. Peel and cut each quarter across in half, to make eight pieces in all. Wrap half a rindless bacon rasher around each piece of avocado and thread on to skewers. Cook near the coals for 5 – 6 minutes, turning once, until the bacon is cooked. Serve at once, enough for two.

B

BAKED BEANS

Bean Bonanza

Cook over the hob as an accompaniment to barbecued food, or prepare in advance and heat through over the barbecue. Cook 1 finely chopped onion, 100 g/4 oz chopped rindless bacon and a crushed clove of garlic in 2 tablespoons oil until the onion is soft and bacon cooked. Stir in a 425-g/15-oz can of baked beans in tomato sauce and a 425-g/15-oz can of red kidney beans (drained), and heat gently. Chilli powder may be added to the onion mixture if liked – about ¼ teaspoon.

BANANAS

Place whole bananas on the cooking rack and leave until the skin turns black underneath – about 2–5 minutes depending on the heat of the coals. Turn and cook the second side until black. Bananas cook well even when the coals look as though they are quite dead – just move the cooking rack to the lowest position and leave the bananas a little longer. Cut two slits along the top of each banana and remove a strip of skin. Trickle pure maple syrup into the banana and use a teaspoon to scoop out the fruit – yum!

Instead of maple syrup, top the bananas with clotted or whipped cream, or ice cream. Add grated chocolate, chopped walnuts or hazelnuts, or trickle over a little warmed raspberry jam.

BARBECUE SAUCE

Prepare in advance to accompany barbecued food. Cook a finely chopped onion and 2 crushed cloves of garlic in 2 tablespoons oil over low heat until soft but not browned – about 10 minutes. Stir in 4 tablespoons tomato purée, 2 tablespoons mild mustard (wholegrain is good, otherwise Dijon or Swedish), 2 teaspoons Worcestershire sauce, 2 table-spoons cider vinegar, 2 tablespoons soft brown sugar and 150 ml/¼ pint water. Stir until boiling, then simmer for 5 minutes to thicken slightly. Serve with chicken, beef, lamb, pork, gammon, sausages or burgers. May also be brushed thinly over food before barbecuing.

BASS

Ask the fishmonger to gut the fish, leaving the head on. Rinse and dry the fish, then sprinkle the body cavity with salt, freshly ground black pepper and a squeeze of lemon juice. Place sprigs of parsley or dill in the cavity and brush the fish all over with oil.

Cook at a medium height over the coals for 10–15 minutes. Use two fish slices, or a large palette knife and fish slice, to turn the fish and cook for a further 10–15 minutes. Lift on to a warmed serving plate, carefully peel off the skin, then use a fork and spoon to serve portions of the fish. Offer soured cream with plenty of chopped dill or chives added.

BAY LEAVES

Place one or two in the body cavity of whole fish (for example, mackerel, trout or mullet). Use bay leaves in a marinade for poultry, beef, lamb or pork before cooking, and lay the leaves on top of the meat or poultry as it barbecues. Thread the leaves on to skewers between other foods when making kebabs.

BEEF

Cook tender steak and good-quality minced beef. Marinate the meat for several hours or overnight (see Marinades, page 75) if wished. Meat that is not marinated should be seasoned and brushed with oil. Baste the meat during cooking, either with oil or with marinade. As a general guide, if you like a rare steak, with the outside browned but the meat bloody, place the cooking rack near the coals. Thin steak may be cooked near the coals, for example minute steaks which are good steaks beaten out until very thin. Thicker, larger steaks should be cooked at a medium height above the coals to prevent the outside browning too quickly. Large, thick steaks (such as T-bone steaks) should be cooked quite high above the coals for a well-done result. The following is a guide to cooking times for different steaks:

Fillet steak (thick)	*– 8–15 minutes*
Minute steak	*– 5–8 minutes*
Rump steak (medium–thick)	*– 7–10 minutes*
T-bone steak (thick)	*– 14–25 minutes*

Fillet, minute and rump steaks should be turned halfway through cooking. T-bone steak should be turned often to prevent the outside from overcooking.

Serve the cooked steak topped with a pat of savoury butter – Anchovy Butter, page 28, or Maître d'Hôtel Butter, page 29. Alternatively, serve Horseradish Cream Sauce (page 60).

Steak Kebabs

Cut 450 g/1 lb rump steak into 2.5 cm/1 in cubes. Mix 2 tablespoons mild wholegrain mustard, 4 tablespoons olive oil, 4 tablespoons dry sherry, salt and pepper. Put the meat and 8 bay leaves in a basin, add the mustard marinade and mix well. Cover and leave for at least 2 hours, preferably chill overnight.

Peel 12 pickling onions and blanch in boiling water for 1 minute. Drain and thread on to four skewers with the meat and bay leaves. Cook well above the coals, basting and turning often, for 15–20 minutes.

See also Hamburgers (page 57).

BLACKBERRY PARCELS

A cheap and cheerful dessert. The fruit is not cooked but just heated through with honey and orange. Good with cream or thick yogurt.

Divide 450 g/1 lb large, juicy blackberries between four pieces of foil. Mix the rind and juice of 1

orange with 2 tablespoons honey.
Spoon this over the blackberries,
close the foil tightly and place the
parcels on the cooking rack. Leave
for 10–15 minutes.

BLACK PUDDING

Good for brunch barbecues! Cut thick slices of black
pudding and push skewers through them so that the cut
side will sit flat on the cooking rack. The slices may be
placed directly on the cooking rack but they are easier
to turn on skewers. Brush with a little oil and cook fairly
near the coals for 5–7 minutes, turning once. Good with
bacon rolls and Apple Sauce (page 20) as accompaniments.

BRATWURST

A fine-textured German pork sausage. Most are sold
cooked, readly for grilling; fresh bratwurst must be
simmered for about 5 minutes before grilling. Barbecue
at a medium height over the coals, allowing about 4–5
minutes on each side.

BREAD

Warm pitta bread or nan by placing on the cooking rack
for about 30 seconds, then turning over to heat the
second side. Line a basket with a hot, clean tea-towel to
wrap the bread and keep it hot.

Crusty French bread or rolls may be warmed to one
side of the barbecue or on the warming rack. Granary,
wholemeal or rye bread also go well with barbecued
food.

See also Garlic Bread plus variations (page 54).

BRIQUETTES

Pre-formed charcoal briquettes are even in size and shape. They tend to take longer to light than ordinary lumpwood charcoal but they are supposed to burn longer and more evenly. I did not notice any particular difference in the burning times. However, lumpwood charcoal is uneven in size, with some very large chunks that are difficult and messy to break.

If you are lighting a large, deep barbecue, then lumpwood charcoal is best; if you have a fairly small barbecue, the briquettes are a better size as they fit together well to give a good, solid heat source without needing to have any great depth.

BUCK'S FIZZ

Combine one-third chilled fresh orange juice with two-thirds chilled champagne or sparkling dry white wine. Serve in tall glasses.

BUTTERS

Flavoured butters, both savoury and sweet, make excellent accompaniments to barbecued foods. Form the flavoured butter into a roll on a piece of foil. Chill well, then cut into slices. Try some of the following ideas.

Anchovy Butter

Mash a 50 g/2 oz can of anchovies with their oil, a squeeze of lemon juice and some freshly ground black pepper. Gradually work the anchovy mixture into 175 g/6 oz butter. Good with beef steak, aubergines or hamburgers.

Garlic Butter

Cream 1 crushed clove of garlic with 100 g/4 oz butter, adding a little salt and pepper if wished. Serve with beef and lamb steaks, cutlets or chops; fresh tuna steaks; Mediterranean prawns; large mushrooms or vegetable kebabs.

Herb Butter

Cream 100 g/4 oz butter with 4–6 tablespoons chopped fresh herbs. Include some parsley, a little thyme, chives, a little sage and/or rosemary, tarragon and other herbs as available. Use small amounts of strong herbs and larger quantities of delicate ones.

Alternatively, flavour the butter with just one herb – tarragon, chives, rosemary, parsley, basil or lemon balm.

Lemon Butter, savoury

Cream 100 g/4 oz butter with the grated rind of 1 lemon and 1 tablespoon chopped parsley. Serve with fish, poultry or vegetables.

Lemon Butter, sweet

Omit the parsley used above and beat 1 tablespoon honey into the butter. Unsalted butter is best and extra honey may be added to taste. Good with barbecued bananas and fruit kebabs.

Maître d'Hôtel Butter

Cream 100 g/4 oz butter with a good squeeze of lemon juice, 3 tablespoons chopped parsley and seasoning to taste. Good with all fish, poultry, meat and vegetables.

Nut Butter, savoury

Beat 50 g/2 oz finely chopped walnuts or hazelnuts, 2 tablespoons snipped chives and freshly ground black pepper into 100 g/4 oz butter. Good with chicken, turkey, pork, Red Lentil Croquettes (page 71) or Chick Pea Patties (page 35).

Nut Butter, sweet

Combine nuts and butter as above, omitting other ingredients and adding 3 tablespoons icing sugar with 2 tablespoons brandy. Use to fill Baked Apples (page 19) or in Blackberry Parcels (page 26).

Olive Butter

Stone and chop 10 black olives, then mix with 100 g/4 oz butter. Add 1 small crushed clove of garlic if liked. Serve with lamb, aubergines, duck breasts, Red Lentil Croquettes (page 71) or Chick Pea Patties (page 35).

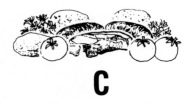

C

CHARCOAL

The fuel for the majority of barbecues. It varies from great lumps down to small chips; you may have to break up the large pieces. Keep charcoal dry and pack it in a sealed polythene bag if you are keeping it for several months.

CHEESE

Goat's Cheese in Vine Leaves

Wrap a small whole goat's cheese with herbs and garlic in 2 or 3 vine leaves. Skewer the leaves in place, brush with oil and cook for 3–4 minutes on each side. Serve with warm crusty bread.

Grilled Halloumi

A tough sheep's cheese. Cut it into large chunks or slices, marinate overnight in olive oil and chopped fresh oregano or marjoram (add garlic if you like), then allow the oil to drip off before threading chunks on to skewers and grilling for 2–3 minutes on each side until brown and crisp. The cheese will be soft and moist inside.

> ▶ Include halloumi or feta cheese in vine leaves on vegetable kebabs. Good with mushrooms and tomatoes because they all cook quickly.

Cheese Boats

Halve peppers lengthways, scoop out all the seeds and grill them cut side down for 5 minutes to soften slightly. Brush the skin side with a little oil and put a slice of ripe brie or similar soft cheese in each half. Grill skin side down for 2–4 minutes, until browned and the cheese is melting. Season with freshly ground pepper and top with chopped peeled tomato to serve.

Raclette

A Swiss cheese which is melted in front of the fire, then the middle is scraped on to plates and eaten with baked potatoes, gherkins and sliced raw onion. You may find raclette in a good cheese shop, in which case you will need a large chunk to melt over the barbecue (traditionally a half cheese would be used).

CHICK PEAS

These have a nutty flavour that stands up to barbecuing or goes well with barbecued food.

Hummus

A really tasty dip to keep hunger pangs at bay. Drain a 425-g/15-oz can of chick peas and place in a food processor with 1 slice onion, 1 clove of garlic (peeled) and a squeeze of lemon juice. Process until finely chopped. Measure 150 ml/¼ pint olive oil. Add a little to the chick peas with 2 tablespoons tahini (sesame paste). Process until the mixture begins to form a paste. Scrape it down into the bowl and process, adding the remaining olive oil very slowly. The mixture will form a soft, creamy paste. Season, adding extra lemon juice if liked.

If you do not have a food processor, finely chop the onion, crush the garlic and mash the chick peas. Beat well with a little oil and the tahini, then continue beating, adding the oil drop by drop.

Chick Pea Patties

Drain two 425-g/15-oz cans of chick peas. Cook 1 finely chopped onion with 1 crushed clove of garlic in 2 tablespoons olive oil until soft but not browned. Mash the chick peas, add to the pan and remove from the heat. Mix in 50 g/2 oz fresh wholemeal breadcrumbs, salt and pepper, 2 tablespoons tahini, 4 tablespoons chopped parsley, 1 teaspoon chopped fresh mint and a squeeze of lemon juice. Press the mixture together, shape into eight small round cakes and chill if there is time. Brush with a little oil before grilling for 3–4 minutes on each side, until golden.

Chick Pea Salad

Soak dried chick peas overnight, then drain and boil them for about 1 hour until tender. Mix with 3 finely chopped spring onions, 1 finely chopped green pepper (remove all seeds and pith first), 6 peeled and chopped tomatoes, 4 tablespoons olive oil, 2 tablespoons lemon juice, salt and pepper, a crushed clove of garlic (if liked) and lots of chopped parsley (pick a big bunch or chop up a whole packet). Mix well, leave to marinate for 1 hour, then serve in Iceberg lettuce leaves if you like.

CHICKEN

Tender chicken barbecues well. It must be cooked right through before serving. Cut several slits into the thickest part of the chicken flesh and marinate it for a few hours or overnight if liked (see Marinades, page 75). The slits allow the flesh to absorb flavours and to cook through more efficiently. Cook chicken at a medium height over the coals (or quite high) so that it cooks through before over-browning. Turn frequently. The following times are a guide for different portions.

Boneless or part-boned *chicken breasts*	*– 20–25 minutes*
Drumsticks	*– 35–40 minutes*
Chicken thighs	*– 35–40 minutes*
Chicken quarters *or halved chickens*	*– 35–45 minutes*
Whole chicken (spit-roasted)	*– 1¹/₄–1¹/₂ hours*

★ **HERBS** Thyme, lemon thyme or balm, rosemary, sage and tarragon all complement chicken. For the simplest marinade, sprinkle plenty of fresh herbs over the chicken, drizzle over a little oil and lemon juice and add seasoning. Cover and chill.

Lemon Chicken

Mix the grated rind and juice of 1 lemon with plenty of chopped parsley, 1 teaspoon honey, seasoning and 150 ml/¼ pint fromage frais. Skin four boneless chicken breasts and marinate in the lemon mixture before grilling.

Tandoori Chicken

Crush 3 large cloves of garlic into 150 ml/¼ pint natural yogurt. Add

2 tablespoons oil, 1 teaspoon turmeric, 2 tablespoons ground coriander, 1 tablespoon ground cumin, ½ teaspoon chilli powder, 1 teaspoon each of ground ginger and cinnamon, the juice of 1 lemon, salt and pepper. Marinate 8 chicken thighs overnight in the mixture before grilling for 35–40 minutes. Brush often with the marinade during cooking.

Chicken Kebabs

Cut 450 g/1 lb boneless chicken breast into thick chunks. Place in a bowl. Add 2 tablespoons oil, 1 teaspoon dried marjoram, 1 teaspoon tomato purée, salt and pepper and mix well. Leave to marinate. Thread on to four metal skewers with bay leaves and pieces of green pepper. Cook for 20–25 minutes, turning often, until cooked through.

Oriental Chicken Wings

Mix 4 tablespoons soy sauce, 2 teaspoons sesame oil, 1 teaspoon sugar, 1 crushed clove of garlic and 2 tablespoons finely chopped fresh root ginger. Spoon over 8 chicken wings and marinate overnight. Grill for 25–30 minutes, until crisp and brown, brushing often with the marinade. Serve with shredded spring onion, allowing two wings per person.

▶ Part-cook chicken pieces in the microwave before cooking them on the barbecue. This way the chicken cooks through quickly on the barbecue and it has an excellent flavour.

For a barbecue party, cook the chicken drumsticks in a baking tray covered with foil in the conventional oven – keep the oven temperature at about 180°C/350°F/gas 4, or lower, so that the chicken does not brown. Check that the drumsticks are cooked. They may be cooked the day before, cooled and refrigerated overnight. Sprinkle with herbs or other flavourings and brown on the barbecue, allowing about 5–7 minutes on each side so that they are hot through. They taste good and you can be sure they are cooked through.

CHINESE LEAVES

These make a good crisp salad. Hold the head by the stalk end and cut across the other end, working about halfway down the length of the vegetable to shred the leaves finely. Wash, then drain and dry.

Cut 4 celery sticks into 5-cm/2-in lengths, then cut each piece lengthways into fine sticks. Place in a bowl of iced water for 15–20 minutes. Mix the celery, Chinese leaves, 2 chopped spring onions and a finely diced yellow or red pepper (all seeds and pith removed). Roast 50 g/2 oz flaked almonds in a small, heavy pan without any oil until golden. Toss into the salad.

CHIVES

Wash chives, then snip them into small pieces with scissors. Add to salads or marinades. Good with fish and chicken.

Chive Dip

Mix 4 tablespoons snipped chives with 150 ml/¼ pint mayonnaise (buy a good one that does not taste tart). Stir in salt and pepper to taste, ½ teaspoon paprika and 150 ml/¼ pint thick natural yogurt (the very creamy Greek yogurt is good).

CHORIZO

Spicy Spanish sausages seasoned with paprika. Cook them whole on the barbecue until well browned outside – about 10 minutes, turning often. Delicious with a Chick Pea Salad (page 36).

Chorizo Kebabs

Cut 4 chorizo into chunks. Peel and blanch 16 pickling onions in boiling water for 2 minutes. Drain. Scrub and cook 16 new potatoes until just tender. Thread the chorizo, onions and potatoes on to four metal skewers. Brush with olive oil and cook at a medium height over the coals for 10 minutes, turning two or three times, until evenly browned. Serve with soured cream flavoured with chives.

CIDER

Cider Punch

In a large bowl mix a sliced orange, sliced lemon and 150 ml/ ¼ pint medium sherry. Leave for at least an hour, preferably several so that the fruit flavours the sherry. Add a cored, quartered and sliced eating apple, a few slices of cucumber, a bottle (1 litre/1¾ pints) of medium-sweet cider, plenty of ice cubes and sparkling mineral water to taste.

Cider Marinade

Mix 1 tablespoon wholegrain mustard with salt and pepper, 8 tablespoons medium-sweet or dry cider, a bay leaf, slice of onion and 2 tablespoons sunflower oil. Use for chicken, fish (particularly mackerel) and pork.

CLEANING

Brush out cold ashes. Brush cooking racks with a wire brush (special barbecue brushes are available) and wash them in hot soapy water after use. Store in a clean place.

★ *DE-GREASING CLEANER* To remove burnt-on grease.

★ *GAS BARBECUES* Some manufacturers suggest closing the barbecue and burning residue off the cooking racks, cooling and brushing. This is very successful. Remove the cooking racks to wash and dry once all the worst fat has burnt off.

COCONUT

Thread chunks of fresh coconut on to skewers and toast

them over the barbecue until golden. Good to munch with fresh fruit instead of dessert.

Coconut Crunchies

Crumble 175 g/6 oz plain cake into a bowl. Add 100 g/4 oz desiccated coconut and the grated rind of 1 orange. Stir in 2 tablespoons sherry and enough orange juice to bind the mixture. Shape into balls about the size of walnuts and thread metal skewers through them. Press the mixture firmly on to the skewers and grill for about 2 minutes on each side until golden.

COD

Buy cod from the thick end of the fillet so that it can be cut into chunks and threaded on to skewers. Cod steaks also barbecue well.

Cod and Bacon Kebabs

Prepare the fish as above, wrapping each chunk in a half rasher of rindless streaky bacon. Thread on to skewers and cook for about 15 minutes on each side, until the bacon is brown and crisp and the fish cooked. Best to cook mushrooms or other vegetables on separate skewers.

Fish Kebabs

Take 575 g/1¼ lb thick cod fillet. Skin it and cut into chunks. Fold portions from the thin part of the fillet in half to form chunks. You should have about 16 chunks. Wash 16 bay leaves and wipe 16

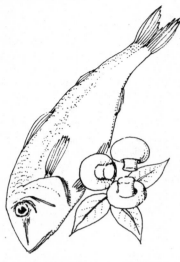

Cod Steaks with Lime and Ginger

button mushrooms. Thread the fish, bay leaves and mushrooms on to four metal skewers. Mix the juice of ½ lemon with salt and freshly ground black pepper, 4 tablespoons sunflower oil, 2 tablespoons chopped parsley or tarragon and a little grated nutmeg. Brush this all over the kebabs and grill for 3–4 minutes at a medium height over the coals. Use a slice to ease the pieces of fish off the cooking rack and turn the kebabs. Cook for 3–4 minutes on the second side. The fish should be lightly browned and firm but still moist when cut. Serve at once.

Leave the skin on four 225-g/8-oz cod steaks. Peel and thinly slice 25 g/1 oz fresh root ginger, then cut it into fine shreds. Cut 2 spring onions into fine shreds and add to the ginger with the grated rind and juice of 1 lime. Stir in 1 tablespoon light soy sauce, a little seasoning and 2 tablespoons oil. Spoon this all over the fish and leave to marinate for 1–2 hours. Place the steaks on the barbecue and spoon the ginger and spring onions over. Cook for 4–5 minutes, until browned underneath. Turn carefully using a fish slice, brush with remaining marinade and cook for a further 4–5 minutes, until firm, cooked through and juicy. Serve at once.

COLESLAW

I love good homemade coleslaw with some apple and raisins added – it tastes terrific with fairly plain grilled foods and baked potatoes. Most of the bought types are far too tart and they bear no comparison to the proper salad.

Remove the hard core from a quarter of a medium-sized white cabbage, then shred it finely. (Easier if you own a food processor!) Grate 4 medium carrots. Halve a small onion, then cut it into very fine slices and separate them into shreds. Peel, core and chop 2 eating apples. Mix all the ingredients, adding 25–50 g/1–2 oz plump raisins (whether you want a hint of raisin or lots is up to you). Sprinkle with 2 tablespoons lemon juice, then add 150 ml/¼ pint good mayonnaise (not a tangy one) and plenty of freshly ground black pepper with salt to taste.

CORNED BEEF

Good for impromptu barbecues!

Hash Cakes

Peel, cook and mash 1 potato. Finely chop 1 onion and cook it in a knob of butter until soft but not browned. Mix well with the potato, a 200-g/7-oz can of corned beef, 75 g/3 oz fresh breadcrumbs, 2 teaspoons horseradish sauce, salt and pepper. Cool, then place in the freezer for 15 minutes to chill. Form the mixture into eight cakes and coat in plenty of flour. If you like, coat as well in egg and fine dry breadcrumbs and chill briefly in the freezer. Brush with oil and place on the barbecue for 4–5 minutes, until crisp and browned underneath. Brush the tops of the cakes with oil and use a slice to turn them carefully. Cook the second side for 4–5 minutes. Lift carefully on to plates and serve with a salad or Bean Bonanza (page 23).

CORN-ON-THE-COB

Roast the whole cobs of corn. Peel back but do not remove the outer husks. Discard the silky hairs from around the corn and rinse well. Brush with a little oil or melted butter and replace the husks. Roast at a medium height over the coals for 30–40 minutes, turning often. Serve at once with a savoury butter (page 30). These make a good starter or accompaniment.

Skewered Corn

Remove all husks and the silky covering from the cobs, then cook them in boiling water for 20–30 minutes until tender. Slice and thread on to skewers. Brush with melted butter and grill for about 2–3 minutes on each side. Skewer with other vegetables to make tasty kebabs. Serve with a savoury butter (page 30) or soured cream.

Baby Corn

Skewer lightly cooked fresh or drained canned baby corn cobs as above.

COURGETTES

Trim ends, halve lengthways and brush with olive oil. Cook skin side down for 3 minutes, then turn and cook the cut side for 2–3 minutes, until browned. Serve with freshly ground black pepper, butter and a squeeze of lemon juice.

Skewered Courgettes

Trim and cut into chunks. Marinate in oil with a sprinkling of oregano or marjoram and freshly ground black pepper. Skewer and grill for 5–6 minutes, turning often. Serve with lemon. See also Vegetable Kebabs (page 120).

Courgette Salad

Select small, very fresh courgettes. Trim and peel off a thin layer of skin, leaving the courgettes a good dark green. Slice thinly and toss with a little shredded lettuce and snipped chives. Dress with olive oil, salt and freshly ground black pepper and a squeeze of lemon juice.

Courgettes with Basil

Combine coarsely grated courgettes with shredded basil leaves, some freshly ground black pepper, a little olive oil and lemon juice. Season very lightly with salt and serve as a salad or as a first course, with crusty bread.

CRUDITÉS

Bite-sized pieces of raw vegetables. Cut carrots, celery, celeriac and peppers into small sticks. Place in iced water with lemon juice added and leave until just before serving. Drain and dry on absorbent kitchen paper when ready to serve; this way they stay really crunchy. Cut cucumber and courgettes into sticks just before serving. Add cherry tomatoes (wash them but leave their stalks on), wedges of apple, grapes, wedges of fresh peach. Cut apples and peaches at the last minute and toss in lemon juice to prevent them discolouring. Serve crudités with dips (see pages 45–47).

CUCUMBER

Peel lightly, slice very thinly and spread out on a platter. Sprinkle with a little salt and freshly ground black pepper, drizzle over some very light oil (try grapeseed), then add a squeeze of lemon or lime juice. To make the salad more exciting, sprinkle with shredded fresh basil or add slices of strawberry (or both, they go together very well). Particularly good with lamb or hamburgers.

Tsatziki

A Greek starter that is wonderful on hot days. Grate ½ cucumber, place in a sieve and sprinkle with salt. Leave over a basin for 30 minutes, then squeeze all the liquid out of the cucumber and place the shreds in a basin. Don't worry if they have formed a dry lump. Add 1 tablespoon very finely chopped onion and a crushed clove of garlic. Stir in 300 ml/ ½ pint chilled Greek yogurt and add a little seasoning to taste.

D

DEVILLED SAUCE

The fiery combination of ingredients gives this sauce its name. Serve it as a relish with hamburgers or sausages or brush it sparingly over meat or poultry before cooking.

Finely chop 1 onion and cook it with 2 crushed cloves of garlic in 3 tablespoons oil until soft but not browned. Stir in 1 teaspoon flour, a good pinch of cayenne pepper, 2 teaspoons ground coriander, 3 tablespoons wholegrain mustard, 2 tablespoons tomato purée and 1 tablespoon Worcestershire sauce. Add 150 ml/¼ pint medium-sweet cider, stir well and bring to the boil. Boil for about a minute to thicken the sauce slightly, stirring all the time. Taste and adjust the seasoning if necessary.

DIPS

Serve these with crisps or crudités while the main course is cooking. The dips may also be served to accompany plain grilled foods. Each of the following serves four.

Anchovy Dip   Mash a 50 g/2 oz can of anchovies with their oil. Add a finely chopped spring onion, the grated rind of ½ lemon and a good squeeze of lemon juice. Stir in 100 g/4 oz soft cheese (quark, curd cheese or cream cheese) and 150 ml/¼ pint Greek yogurt or mayonnaise.

Blue Cheese Dip

Mash 100 g/4 oz Danish blue cheese with 1 tablespoon lemon juice, then stir in 150 ml/¼ pint soured cream or thick yogurt. Add freshly ground black pepper to taste.

Garlic Mayonnaise

Crush a fresh, plump clove of garlic and add 300 ml/½ pint homemade, or good-quality bought, mayonnaise. Sprinkle with a little paprika before serving. For a spicy alternative make a quick rouille by adding 1 teaspoon paprika and stirring in a good pinch of cayenne.

Guacamole

Mash 1 large ripe avocado. Beat in a little lemon juice, a small crushed clove of garlic, a good pinch of chilli powder and seasoning. Peel, deseed and chop 2 ripe tomatoes, stir them into the avocado mixture with 150 ml/¼ pint soured cream. Season to taste and add more chilli powder if you like. Serve with tortilla chips and crudités.

Herb Dip

Chop a good bunch of fresh herbs – parsley, a little mint, basil, some oregano or marjoram, a small sprig of rosemary, fennel and just a little thyme. Mix with 100 g/4 oz cream cheese, 150 ml/¼ pint mayonnaise and seasoning to taste. Chill before serving.

Tomato and Onion Dip

Finely chop a large Spanish onion, then cook it over a low heat in 25 g/1 oz butter for about 15 minutes, stirring occasionally, until really soft but not browned. Cool. Peel, deseed and chop 4 ripe tomatoes. Add to the onion with 2 tablespoons chopped parsley. Stir in 100 g/4 oz low-fat soft cheese, 150 ml/¼ pint fromage frais and seasoning to taste. Chill before serving.

See also Hummus (page 34) and Tsatziki (page 44).

DUCK

Barbecued duck is delicious but it does demand attention during cooking, otherwise the fat content can cause flare ups. Trim off lumps of fat before cooking and marinate duck for the best flavour. Cook it fairly high above the heat so that it has plenty of time to cook through and become crisp. Turn the duck often during cooking. The following times are a guide to cooking – try some of the flavouring suggestions that follow.

Duck halves or quarters – 1 hour
Boneless duck breasts – 20–25 minutes

Orange and Rosemary Duck

Sprinkle duck portions with chopped rosemary and the grated rind of an orange. Pour over the orange juice, add seasoning to taste and marinate for several hours. Cook the duck and heat the marinade separately, adding 2 tablespoons redcurrant or crab apple jelly. When the jelly has dissolved and the marinade boils, brush it over the cooked duck and serve.

Spiced Duck

Mix 2 tablespoons ground coriander with 1 teaspoon ground ginger and a good pinch of turmeric. Rub the duck portions all over with a cut clove of garlic, the coriander mixture and plenty of salt and pepper. Serve lemon wedges with the cooked duck.

> ▶ Cook a whole duck in the microwave before barbecuing. Place it in a covered dish or roasting bag (tie the bag with a microwave-proof tie), then cook on full power for 20–30 minutes, turning twice and draining off excess fat. Drain and pat dry on absorbent kitchen paper, season well and coat with spices, herbs or other flavourings. Brown on the barbecue until crisp and golden. The duck may be jointed before barbecuing. Delicious!

F

FAT

Fat dripping from food burns and flames on the barbecue, blackening the food or even setting it alight if the barbecue is unattended. Apart from the danger factor, the flavour of the food is ruined.

Trim excess fat from foods before cooking, particularly lumps of fat on poultry and excess fat on chops. When basting food take care not to splash the barbecue. Fatty foods should be cooked fairly high above the heat so that they do not sizzle violently. If the food is very near the heat more fat drips off and the barbecue is more likely to flare up.

An old tin or foil container may be placed between coals under the food to catch the fat. This is not practical when cooking several small cuts of food but it is useful for joints of meat. However, the fat in the tin becomes very hot and it does ignite. Have a water spray at hand (the type used for plants) to douse flames, and have fire tongs ready to remove a tin that has started to flame. Allow the tin to cool, wipe out the fat, then it may be replaced under the joint. The tin should not be too large, so it does not cover the barbecue completely. If the barbecue is very small this is not always practical.

Use long-handled food tongs and a slice to remove food from the cooking rack if the barbecue flares. Setting the food to one side for a few minutes should be sufficient to quell the flames; if not, spray a little water over the charcoal. **Never spray water over a gas or electric barbecue**.

FENNEL

There are three forms of fennel: the herb and the seeds (spice) from the same plant, also the vegetable, or Florence fennel. All types have a similar, aniseed-like flavour.

★ *FENNEL SEEDS* Use these in marinades for meat, poultry or fish. Very good with rich meats such as lamb or pork. Roast the seeds first in a dry, heavy-bottomed pan until they just begin to pop. Mix them with other marinade ingredients or simply sprinkle them over the food before cooking.

★ *FENNEL HERB* Green and feathery, this has a delicate aniseed flavour. It is excellent with fish; sprigs may be put in the body cavity of whole fish or rolled up in fillets. The chopped herb may be sprinkled over food.

★ *FENNEL BULBS* Plump bulbs of fennel are about the size of medium potatoes or apples. They may be cooked or eaten raw. Try this refreshing salad.

Fennel and Orange Salad

Finely shred a fennel bulb. Cut all peel and pith from 2 oranges then cut between the membranes to remove the segments. Squeeze all juice from the membranes before discarding. Mix 2 finely chopped spring onions and a shredded lettuce heart with the fennel. Add the orange segments. Whisk a little sugar and seasoning into the juice of a third orange plus all the reserved juice, then gradually whisk in olive oil. Toss this into the salad.

FIRELIGHTERS

These are used to help ignite the barbecue. Place in between the charcoal before lighting, following the packet instructions.

FISH

Small whole fish barbecue well, for example sardines, herrings, trout and mackerel. The oily fish tend to flare up during cooking, so they do need special attention. Since all fish has a delicate texture, care must be taken when turning it to avoid breaking the flesh. A special cooking rack that encloses the fish is best for sardines and herrings and it also eases the cooking of other whole fish.

Use firm fish for kebabs – cod, swordfish, huss or monkfish. Fish steaks also cook well but fillets can be difficult as they tend to break up easily. For success, the cooking rack must be clean and the pieces of fish should be brushed with a little oil (or a marinade containing oil). Have a long-handled metal slice to turn fish during cooking and ease the edges off the cooking rack before sliding the slice underneath. Make sure the fish is loosened from the cooking rack before flipping it over.

Always brush fish with a basting liquid during cooking as it does tend to dry out. Fish may also be wrapped in foil and cooked on the barbecue. Try mackerel or trout in foil, adding herbs and lemon to flavour it during cooking.

See also Cod (page 39), Mackerel (page 74), Plaice (page 90), etc.

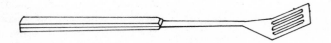

▶ Try barbecuing fish fingers – brush with oil and cook from frozen. Frozen or homemade fish cakes (coated with egg and breadcrumbs) also barbecue well, but not too near the heat if they are frozen, so that they thaw properly and cook through.

FISH RACK

Hinged, fish-shaped rack, to hold and turn fish during cooking. To hold one or more fish. Oblong or square racks may be used instead.

FOIL

Used to wrap some foods. Always use a heavy-duty foil or double thinner foils so they do not rip easily.

FRANKFURTERS

Ready cooked, these barbecue quickly. They may be cooked near the heat, at a medium height or high: the nearer they are to the heat, the quicker they brown. At a medium height allow about 2 minutes on each side, until browned. Serve in warm finger rolls with Coleslaw (page 41), relish, chutney or ketchup.

Frankfurter Kebabs

Skewer chunks of frankfurter with vegetables that cook quickly: mushrooms, tomatoes, pieces of pepper and canned baby sweet-corn. Add pieces of canned pine-apple, apple, orange or fresh peach. Brush with a little oil and season or use one of the marinades (page 75) to baste the kebabs.

FRUIT

Fruit Kebabs

Skewer chunks of fruit, brush with a little melted butter and cook over the barbecue, fairly high above the coals, for 2–3 minutes on each side, until hot but not mushy. Try chunks of eating apple, banana slices, chunks of peeled orange (remove pips), chunks of fresh or canned pineapple, halved and stoned plums, chunks of peach, halved and stoned apricots, and large strawberries.

Fruit Packets

Instead of kebabs combine bite-sized pieces of fruit (any of the above) and mound them on large pieces of foil. Fold the foil up, sprinkle the fruit with a little brandy, sherry, liqueur or juice (orange, pineapple, passion fruit or apple) and close the foil tightly. Heat on the barbecue for about 5–7 minutes, longer over dying charcoal.

G

GAMMON

Barbecue gammon steaks quite high over the heat, turning often, for 17–20 minutes, until browned and cooked through. Baste with Orange Marinade (page 83) during cooking.

Gammon Kebabs

Skewer 2.5-cm/1-in chunks of gammon – 450 g/1 lb for four kebabs. Chunks of onion or small whole onions may be added, also bay leaves. Do not overfill skewers as the meat must be evenly cooked – any chunks right at the end of the skewers may not cook properly if they sit over the edge of the cooking area. Mix 1 tablespoon honey, 2 tablespoons apple juice, 1 tablespoon oil, ½ teaspoon chopped fresh sage and freshly ground black pepper to taste. Brush over the kebabs and cook for about 20 minutes, turning often, until well browned and cooked through.

GARLIC BREAD

Prepare Garlic Butter (page 29). Cut a French loaf into slices, leaving them attached at the base. Spread the butter on the slices and press back together. Wrap in foil and place at the side or back of the barbecue (or in the warming drawer of those barbecues that have one). The bread should be hot in about 10 minutes.

Alternatively, use other flavours instead of garlic (page 28), or add plenty of fresh herbs to the garlic butter.

GAS BARBECUES

Use high, medium or low heat settings instead of

moving the cooking rack down or up. These cook evenly, with greater control than charcoal barbecues. Foods that cook very quickly do not have as good a flavour but meat, chicken and other foods that require longer cooking taste good. Marinating and basting are very important. See also Smoking (page 111); place the smoking ingredients on a small foil container and pierce all over the base. For the best flavour cook with the barbecue lid on – this is also quicker.

Gas barbecues are ideal for impromptu winter cooking. Even if you are eating inside use this appliance for cooking delicious meals.

GINGER

A versatile spice for flavouring savoury and sweet foods. An excellent ingredient for marinades, fresh root ginger may be peeled and shredded, then sprinkled over fish or chicken. Barbecue after several hours' marinating, then serve with shredded spring onions. A sprinkling of ground ginger may be substituted for fresh root ginger, although it lacks the zest of the fresh spice.

Ginger Beer

Here is my mother's recipe for ginger beer. It involves starting a 'ginger beer plant' which is fed every day. She has always had tremendous success with this.

Mix 50 g/2 oz fresh yeast (from a small baker's, health food shop or try a hot bread counter at a big supermarket), 2 teaspoons each of sugar and ground ginger and 300 ml/½ pint lukewarm water in a large jar. Put the lid on top but do not close. Leave for 7–10 days,

Ginger Refresher

adding 1 teaspoon each of ground ginger and sugar every day. Strain the ginger beer plant through scalded muslin, reserving the sediment. To the liquid add 450 g/1 lb sugar, the juice of 2 lemons and 600 ml/1 pint boiling water. Stir until the sugar dissolves, then make up to 4.5 litres/8 pints with cold water. Bottle, leaving a 7.5-cm/3-in space at the top of each bottle. Leave for 2 hours in a warm room, then cover lightly with screw-top caps and store in a cool place for 7–10 days, by which time the ginger beer will be ready to drink.

Divide the reserved sediment in two and put each portion in a jar; to each add 1 teaspoon ground ginger and 1 teaspoon sugar with 300 ml/½ pint water. Bottle, store and open with care. Keep out of children's reach.

Place a sherry glass of ginger wine in a large wine glass. Add 2 tablespoons lime juice, a slice of lime and a couple of ice cubes. Top up with tonic or sparkling mineral water – the first makes a sweeter drink than the second.

GOOSEBERRY FOOL

Place 450 g/1 lb gooseberries in a saucepan with 100 g/4 oz sugar and the grated rind and juice of

1 orange. The orange goes well but it is not essential. Heat gently until the sugar has dissolved, then simmer the fruit, covered, for about 15 minutes, stirring occasionally, until pulpy. Sieve or purée in a food processor or liquidizer and press through a sieve. Set aside to cool. Either mix the fruit purée into 600 ml/1 pint chilled custard (homemade or canned) or fold in 300 ml/½ pint double cream, whipped until thick. Transfer to serving dishes and chill well.

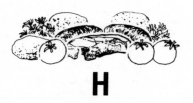

H

HAMBURGERS

Combine 1 kg/2¼ lb minced steak, 50 g/2 oz fresh breadcrumbs, ½ teaspoon dried sage, ¼ teaspoon dried thyme, salt and freshly ground black pepper and 1 beaten egg. Pound the mixture together with a wooden spoon. Divide into four or eight portions and shape into flat, round burgers. Brush with a little oil and barbecue the small burgers for about 15 minutes, turning once or twice. Barbecue the large burgers for 20–25 minutes, turning twice.

<u>Steak Burgers</u>

Buy rump steak or good braising steak, trim and mince it. Mix with plenty of seasoning, then divide into 175-g/6-oz or 225-g/8-oz portions. With clean, wet hands, knead each portion of meat into a neat, round burger, pressing it together well in the palm of your hand first – it is this 'kneading' or moulding process that keeps the burger in shape. Brush with a little oil and cook over the barbecue until cooked through (20–25 minutes for large ones, 15–20 minutes for the smaller ones), or until cooked to your liking.

▶ Frozen burgers may be barbecued – cooking times vary with size and fat content. Very fatty burgers cause flare ups, so take care!
  As well as all the supermarket and frozen brands, if you have a good local butcher ask if he makes his own burgers – you may be surprised at the quality. My butcher makes beef burgers and steak burgers, the latter being all meat. They taste better than the majority of branded burgers and they are a far better buy in terms of price per pound!

HERBS

Herbs are the great ally of the barbecue cook. It goes

without saying that fresh are best and they are readily available from most supermarkets. It is also easy to grow herbs in pots. Sprinkle chopped fresh herbs over foods before cooking, add them to marinade mixtures, toss into salads or burn them on the barbecue.

Burn rosemary or other woody herbs on the barbecue to give the food a wonderful flavour. On a gas or electric barbecue, pack the sprigs of herbs in foil and pierce it all over before placing directly on the heated base.

★ *BAY LEAVES* Use when marinating food, thread on to kebabs or burn them on hot coals.

★ *MARJORAM* Similar to oregano, not quite as strong. This is good with pork, beef, lamb and vegetables.

★ *MINT* A strong herb, use in small amounts when mixed with other herbs. Sprinkle over grilled lamb. Good in salads and with vegetables.

★ *OREGANO* Similar to marjoram but slightly stronger. Good with all vegetables, poultry, fish and meat.

★ *PARSLEY* Use with all foods, in marinades or sprinkled over after cooking. Excellent in green salads.

★ *ROSEMARY* A strong herb, good with lamb, pork, chicken or fish such as mackerel. Burn sprigs on the barbecue to give food an excellent flavour.

★ *SAGE* Use with pork, burgers and chicken. A strong herb with a peppery flavour.

★ *SAVORY* Small-leafed herb similar in flavour to thyme. Quite strong. Use with all meat and poultry and with mackerel, or sparingly with other fish.

★ *THYME* Strongly flavoured, this may be used carefully with fish, poultry, meat and vegetables.

HERRINGS

Best to use a fish rack to contain these so that they may be turned easily during cooking. Have them gutted, with heads and tails left on. Place a bay leaf in the body cavity of each fish. Sprinkle with salt, freshly ground pepper and lemon juice before grilling for 7–9 minutes, turning once. Cook fairly high above the heat as they can cause flare ups if too near. Good with Mustard Sauce (page 81).

HICKORY CHIPS

Dried chips of hickory wood, from North American trees whose wood is used to smoke food. The chips may be used on charcoal or on gas and electric barbecues. They should be soaked in water, following the manufacturer's instructions, then sprinkled over the burning barbecue. On gas or electric barbecues, the hickory should be wrapped in foil which is pierced all over, then placed on the heat source. The hickory gives off a smoke that flavours the food as it cooks; the most pronounced flavour is obtained in a covered barbecue. Hickory is usually used by the handful and is put on the barbecue halfway through cooking. It burns for about 15 minutes.

HORSERADISH

Serve with beef, hamburgers, sausages or mackerel. Buy horseradish sauce or creamed horseradish.

Horseradish Cream Sauce

For a light horseradish sauce, mix 2 tablespoons horseradish sauce with 150 ml/¼ pint soured cream or fromage frais.

HYGIENE

Boring but essential – follow the rules of hygiene when barbecuing.

★ Always wash hands well before handling food.
★ Never leave food uncovered while it is marinating or before it is cooked.
★ Keep all fish and meat chilled until it is to be cooked.
★ Never use the same boards, plates and utensils for cooked and uncooked food. Have warmed clean plates ready to receive the food off the barbecue.
★ Serve barbecued food as soon as it is cooked or cover and keep it hot until it is served.
★ Keep all salads and other foods covered to prevent flies or other insects contaminating them.
★ Thoroughly clean the cooking rack after use.
★ Deal quickly with any leftovers – cover and allow cooked food to cool, then chill as soon as possible.

ICE CREAM

Bought or homemade, ice cream makes an easy dessert. Try this simple recipe or buy good quality ice cream.

Rich Vanilla Ice Cream

Cream 40 g/1½ oz cornflour with 3 egg yolks, 75 g/3 oz sugar, 1 teaspoon natural vanilla essence and a little milk taken from 600 ml/1 pint. Boil the remaining milk, cool slightly, then pour some into the cornflour mixture, stirring. Pour the mixture back into the pan with the remaining milk and heat gently, stirring all the time until the sauce boils and thickens. Cool, covered with cling film or greaseproof paper. Whip 300 ml/ ½ pint double cream until thick, fold into the cooled custard and transfer to a freezer container. Freeze until half frozen, beat well, then replace in the freezer until firm. Make a day in advance.

Serving Ideas

Serve with barbecued bananas (page 23) or with Fruit Packets (page 53).

*   Top with a chocolate sauce made by melting 100 g/4 oz plain chocolate with 4 table-spoons golden syrup and 25 g/1 oz butter in a basin over a saucepan of hot water.
*   Make a hot fruit sauce by blending a little fruit juice taken from 300 ml/½ pint with 3 tablespoons cornflour. Heat the remaining juice, pour on to the cornflour mixture, then return to the pan and bring to the boil. Cook for 2 minutes, stir in sugar to taste and serve. Try pineapple juice, apple juice or any of the other varieties of mixed fruit juice.

ICED TEA

Make some fairly weak tea using Earl Grey or any of the fruit teas that are available. Try orange or strawberry flavoured tea – these are both distinct flavours which are more appealing to those unused to this type of beverage than the anonymous herb or wild fruit teas. Leave to brew for 6–8 minutes, longer for fruit teas, then strain into a bowl and add sugar to taste with slices of lemon. Cool and chill before serving with ice cubes and sprigs of mint.

J

JERUSALEM ARTICHOKES

Thoroughly scrub and remove any bad bits. In a saucepan, cover the artichokes with water and add a good squeeze of lemon juice and a pinch of salt. Simmer gently for about 15 minutes, or until tender. Drain well. Mix 4 tablespoons olive oil with 1 teaspoon grated lemon rind, a little salt and freshly grated nutmeg. Thread the artichokes on to metal skewers, brush with the oil and cook on the barbecue for about 7–10 minutes, turning once or twice until browned and crisp.

JUNIPER BERRIES

Small, round, dark purple berries (at first glance they look almost black), about the size of peppercorns. They give gin its distinctive flavour. Crushed, they may be used in marinades or sprinkled over meat before cooking.

Juniper Marinade

Crush 8 juniper berries in a pestle and mortar. Roast them in a small, heavy-bottomed saucepan over low heat until they give off their aroma and the tiny pieces become firm. Stir during roasting and do not overheat the berries. Remove the pan from the heat and add 4 tablespoons oil – olive or sunflower oil, depending on the flavour required. Stir in 100 ml/ 4 fl oz red wine. Add salt and freshly ground black pepper, a couple of sprigs of parsley and a sprig of thyme.

K

KIDNEYS

Rub the fine membrane and any traces of fat from the outside of lambs' kidneys. Use a pair of kitchen scissors to snip out their cores. Thread the kidneys on to metal skewers, brush with oil and season. Barbecue at a medium height over the coals for about 5–6 minutes on each side. Serve with Devilled Sauce (page 45).

Kidney and Bacon Kebabs

Mix the grated rind of 1 orange with 3 tablespoons sunflower oil, 2 teaspoons fresh thyme leaves (½ teaspoon if using dried) and 2 tablespoons sherry. Season well and pour over 450 g/1 lb prepared lambs' kidneys. Cover and chill for 1 hour. Cut 8 rindless bacon rashers in half, roll up each piece. Thread the bacon rolls and kidneys on to four large metal skewers. Brush with the orange and thyme mixture and cook as above, turning often and basting with the marinade.

KIR ROYALE

Pour a little crème de cassis (blackcurrant liqueur) into a wine glass and top up with well-chilled, sparkling dry white wine.

L

LAMB

Flavour all cuts first with rosemary, mint, garlic, bay leaves, marjoram, oregano or fennel seeds. Red wine, orange juice, olive oil or a little lemon juice are the liquids in which to marinate lamb. Strips of lemon or orange peel also contribute complementary flavours.

Whether lamb should be well cooked or pink in the middle is a matter for personal taste but it should never be cooked until it is dry. The outside should be a rich brown and fat should be crisp. The following times are a guide for different cuts:

Steaks off the leg	*– 9–12 minutes*
Cutlets (trim fat off the bone ends)	*– 11–15 minutes*
Noisettes	*– 12–14 minutes*
Chops (trim fat off the bone ends)	*– 25–35 minutes*
Breast (trim off excess fat, cut into	
ribs and simmer briefly: see below)	*– 12–15 minutes*

Cook lamb at a medium height over the coals, turning it often. Since it yields a lot of fat during cooking take care to prevent the barbecue from flaring up.

Breast of Lamb

Place the prepared ribs in a pan and pour in just enough stock (lamb or chicken) to cover them. Heat gently until simmering, then continue to cook gently for 20 minutes. Drain well. Sprinkle the ribs with plenty of seasoning and herbs or flavourings. They may be marinated at this stage, in a covered dish until cool, then in the refrigerator if left overnight. Brown the ribs at a medium height over the barbecue for 12–15 minutes, turning often. By cooking the lamb first the meat is tender and succulent.

Barbecued Leg of Lamb

The degree of doneness is up to you: if the leg is boned out it may be cooked fairly briefly until thoroughly sealed all over but with the meat still quite bloody. The following method and timings may be used to cook the meat so that it is still pink in the middle or until it is cooked through but still moist.

Trim any lumps of fat off the joint. Make small, fairly deep slits into the meat all over the joint, on the skin side only if boned. Peel and halve cloves of garlic, or quarter them if large. Press pieces of garlic into all the slits. Cut small sprigs of fresh rosemary and press into the slits with the garlic. Rub salt and freshly ground black pepper into the meat, then place it in a dish. Pour over 150 ml/¼ pint red wine and 4 tablespoons olive oil. Cover and chill overnight or for up to 24 hours, turning the joint often and basting with the marinade if possible.

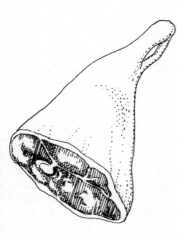

Timing depends on the shape and thickness of the meat as well as weight. For a whole leg weighing about 1.7–1.8 kg/3¾–4 lb, and to cook it through, allow 1½ hours for meat on the bone and up to 1 hour for a boned joint. It is important that the barbecue is ready for cooking in plenty of time and that a charcoal barbecue is large enough to burn for the length of time it takes to cook the lamb. If you have a small barbecue, have hot lumps of charcoal ready to add to it during cooking.

Remove the lamb from the marinade. Make sure that the boned meat will lie flat – it should retain its shape fairly well as the cooking process is slow, but if you have a small joint then push two or three metal skewers horizontally through it to help keep its shape. Cook the lamb high over the coals, turning often and brushing with marinade. Have a small foil tray or tin ready to put between the coals below the lamb to catch dripping fat. Have fire tongs to remove and replace this tin and to rearrange the coals.

If you want the joint pink in the middle, test it after 30–40 minutes. Using a small, sharp pointed knife, make a slit into the thickest part of the joint and check whether the meat is moist and juicy.

▶ Part-cook a leg of lamb conventionally, then finish it off on the barbecue. I have used the microwave to part cook a leg of lamb before putting it on the barbecue and the result was absolutely delicious (the guests never knew that I had cheated). Allow between 8–15 minutes on full power in the microwave (depending on the size of joint), then transfer it to the barbecue. Do not put metal skewers in the microwave.

★ **SHOULDER OF LAMB** Not a good joint to barbecue as it is very fatty.

Lamb Burgers

Follow the method for Hamburgers (page 57), using minced lamb instead of beef. Add 1 teaspoon chopped fresh mint, rosemary or marjoram to the mixture instead of the sage and thyme.

Lamb Kebabs

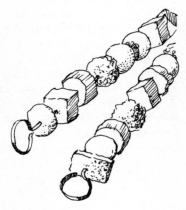

Cut lean boneless lamb, from the fillet or leg, into 2.5-cm/1-in cubes. Marinate in olive oil and a good squeeze of lemon juice, with seasoning, a crushed clove of garlic and a generous sprinkling of chopped fresh marjoram or mint (or a light sprinkling of the dried herb). Best left overnight. Skewer and cook at a medium height, turning two or three times and basting with marinade. Allow about 10–15 minutes, depending on whether you want the lamb pink in the middle or cooked through.

Minced Lamb Kebabs

Mix a grated onion, crushed clove of garlic, 1 tablespoon chopped fresh mint, 1 teaspoon ground coriander and 1 teaspoon ground cinnamon into 675 g/1½ lb minced lamb. Add 25 g/1 oz fresh bread-crumbs and seasoning, then pound the meat so that it binds together. Wet your hands, then take a quarter of the meat and shape in an oval sausage on a metal skewer. The piece of meat should be about 3.75 cm/1½ in long. Press it together firmly on the skewer. Shape the remainder into three more kebabs. Chill for at least 30 minutes before grilling fairly near the coals for 7–10 minutes, turning often until crisp and brown. Serve with wedges of lemon.

LEMON

Serve wedges of lemon with almost any barbecued food.

Lemonade

Thinly peel 4 lemons and squeeze out all their juice. Place the peel in a saucepan with 100 g/4 oz sugar and 150 ml/¼ pint water. Heat slowly, stirring all the time, until the sugar has dissolved. Bring to the boil, add the lemon juice and remove from the heat. Cover, cool and chill. It is best to leave the lemon to infuse in the syrup overnight. Strain the syrup into a large jug and top up with sparkling mineral water. Add a sliced lemon and ice cubes.

Lemon Marinade

Mix the grated rind and juice of 1 lemon with 150 ml/¼ pint oil (olive, sunflower or grapeseed), a bay leaf, 2 sprigs of parsley, a small sprig of thyme, a slice of onion, salt and freshly ground black pepper.

LENTILS

Green Lentil Salad

Cook 225 g/8 oz green lentils in plenty of boiling salted water for 30–35 minutes, until tender. Drain and mix with 4 chopped spring onions, 4 peeled and chopped tomatoes, 1 deseeded and diced red pepper, 4 tablespoons olive oil, 2 tablespoons lemon juice, salt and freshly ground black pepper. Cool. Add plenty of chopped parsley, 1 tablespoon chopped fresh mint and 2 diced avocados just before serving.

Red Lentil Croquettes

Make these in advance to cook over the barbecue. Finely chop 1 onion and cook in 25 g/1 oz butter until just soft. Add 225 g/ 8 oz red lentils and 450 ml/¾ pint water. Bring to the boil, reduce the heat and cover the pan. Simmer for 15–20 minutes, until the water has been absorbed and the lentils are just tender. Continue to cook, uncovered, stirring until the lentils are thick and creamy, about 10 minutes. Transfer to a bowl. Beat in 100 g/4 oz soft cheese (cream cheese, quark or curd cheese), 4 tablespoons chopped parsley and 2 teaspoons chopped fresh marjoram or ½ teaspoon dried marjoram. Add 100 g/4 oz fresh breadcrumbs and season to taste. Cool, then chill. Shape into eight round cakes and coat in flour. Beat an egg with 2 tablespoons water. Coat the cakes in egg and fine dry breadcrumbs, then coat for a second time in egg and breadcrumbs. Chill before cooking. Do this quickly by placing them in the freezer for 10 minutes. Grill at a medium height over the coals for 3–4 minutes on each side.

LIGHTING FLUID

Especially manufactured for lighting charcoal, always follow the manufacturer's instructions. Usually the fluid is squirted over the charcoal, allowed to soak in briefly and then lit. Personally I have not had enormous success with lighting fluid and I find fire lighters (or barbecue lighters) or the sachet-type lighters better.

LIME

Serve lime wedges with savoury barbecued food – the juice complements fish, poultry, meat and vegetables.

Lime Marinade

Mix the grated rind and juice of 1 lime with 4 tablespoons sunflower oil. Add salt and freshly ground black pepper. Use with tarragon for chicken or fish, with a little chopped fresh sage for pork or with 2 tablespoons soy sauce (instead of salt) and 1 tablespoon grated fresh root ginger for Chinese-style chicken, beef, lamb or duck.

LIVER

Lamb's liver barbecues well, either in slices or skewered.

Liver with Orange and Rosemary

Cut 450 g/1 lb lamb's liver into four slices, removing any membrane. Cut three small slits into each piece of liver and spike with small sprigs of rosemary. Place in a dish, add the grated rind and juice of 1 orange, salt, freshly ground black pepper and 2 tablespoons oil. Chill for 1 hour before cooking fairly near the coals for 12–15 minutes, turning once. Brush with the marinade during cooking.

Liver Kebabs

Cut 450 g/1 lb lamb's liver into cubes. Place in a dish and add 2 tablespoons oil, 2 teaspoons wholegrain mustard, 2 tablespoons tomato ketchup, 1 crushed clove of garlic (optional), a good dash of Worcestershire sauce and seasoning. Mix well, cover and chill for 1 hour. Thread on to metal skewers and cook fairly near the coals for 7–10 minutes, brushing with any marinade and turning once or twice.

LOBSTER

Kill a live lobster by placing it in the freezer – leave it there until frozen (overnight). Remove the bands from the claws before cooking the lobster at a medium height over the coals. Turn it often until it is red all over. Use tongs to remove the lobster from the barbecue. Place it on a board and hold it with a clean tea-towel, then use a large, sharp knife to split it through the head and down the back. Remove the gravel sac from the head end of the lobster and remove the black intestinal vein that runs down the length of the body.

Brush with melted butter, sprinkle with a little lemon juice and place cut side down on the barbecue for 3–4 minutes. Serve with wedges of lemon and freshly ground black pepper. Top with pats of Herb, Garlic or Lemon Butter (page 29) if liked. Serve with mayonnaise or soured cream. Use nut crackers to break open the claws, then pick out the meat.

If you buy a ready cooked lobster, halve and prepare as above. Bought, cooked frozen lobsters should be thawed first. When barbecuing bought cooked lobsters, heat them shell down first for 3–4 minutes, then turn and grill to heat through.

M

MACKEREL

Take care with this fish as it may cause the barbecue to flame. Cook it at a medium height over the coals. Small, freshly caught mackerel taste far superior to any from a fishmonger's, so if you visit a small seaside town buy some and freeze them straightaway. Better still, barbecue them on a portable barbecue!

Small Fresh Mackerel

If you do have small fish, gut them, chop off their heads and tails, then wash and dry them on absorbent kitchen paper. Turn them flesh down on a board, run your thumb firmly along the backbone, then turn the fish over and lift away the bones. Dust with plenty of flour and seasoning and place on a perfectly clean cooking rack for about 4 minutes on each side.

Whole Mackerel

'inse gutted mackerel, leaving heads and tails on. Place two bay leaves in each body cavity and season all over. Best cooked in a fish rack. Allow 8–10 minutes, turning once. Serve with lemon.

Mackerel Roll-ups

Use small mackerel, have them cleaned and filleted (the fishmonger will remove the main bones, leaving the fish flesh whole). Cut off any fins and pick out small bones. Cut the mackerel in half lengthways and spread the flesh with horseradish sauce. Season, sprinkle with a little chopped fresh rosemary and roll up from the head end. Thread on to metal skewers and cook for 7–10 minutes, turning carefully.

MARINADES

Marinades are flavouring mixtures in which foods are soaked before cooking. Marinating serves two purposes: firstly it imparts flavour to the food, secondly it helps to tenderize foods such as meat. Acidic ingredients act as tenderizers – for example, citrus or other fruit juices and wine.

Always cover the food and chill it if left for any length of time. Most meats benefit from overnight marinating, similarly poultry. Fish is usually marinated for a few hours and offal is left for a shorter time. Before marinating food make sure that it is very fresh.

Red Wine Marinade

A basic marinade for meat, poultry, strong fish or vegetables such as aubergines, peppers and mushrooms. Place 150 ml/¼ pint red wine in a saucepan and stir in salt to taste, freshly ground black pepper and a pinch of sugar. Add 6 tablespoons oil, a bay leaf, sprig of parsley, sprig of thyme and a halved, peeled clove of garlic (optional). Heat gently until just boiling, then cool before pouring over the food.

White Wine Marinade

A delicate marinade for poultry, fish and vegetables. Mix 150 ml/ ¼ pint dry white wine with a pinch of sugar, salt and freshly ground black pepper. Add 2 good-sized sprigs of parsley, a thin slice of onion and 4 tablespoons sunflower oil. Mix well and pour over the food. Garlic, other herbs or a strip of lemon rind may be added if liked.

MARSHMALLOWS

My skewered marshmallows melted into a disgusting,

sticky mess, coating the barbecue with a nasty-coloured paste. Try toasting them individually, on the end of a skewer or long-handled fork. Hold them just above the cooking rack and whip them away as soon as they show signs of beginning to melt.

MEAT

A few general points:

★ Select tender cuts – stewing meat will not tenderize.
★ Trim off excess fat – too much tends to result in unwanted flames).
★ Marinate meat for best flavour and succulent results.
★ If you are cooking vegetarian food as well as meat, keep the both separate, or cook the vegetarian food before the meat to avoid cross-flavours.
★ Serve freshly cooked.

MELON

Makes a good starter or dessert. Do not skewer on fruit kebabs. For the easiest starter, cut wedges of honeydew melon, remove the seeds, slice across the flesh, and sprinkle with a little chopped preserved ginger to serve. Cut ogen, charentais or other small melons in half, scoop out their seeds and serve just as they are.

MESQUITE

Wood used in America for barbecuing and smoking food.

MINT

There are many types of mint, from the common mint

that grows like a weed to pineapple mint, apple mint, cologne mint (good in punch although too scented for most culinary purposes) or ginger mint. Use with lamb or vegetables and in salads.

Mint Sauce

Dissolve 4 tablespoons caster sugar in 4 tablespoons boiling water. Chop the leaves from a large bunch of mint and add to the sweetened water. Top up with vinegar to taste.

MULLET

Red mullet are ideal for barbecuing as they have fairly tough skin, they are small and they cook quickly. Grey mullet are much larger, although you can sometimes find some about 350 g/12 oz (the size of a large mackerel).

Red Mullet with Bay Leaves

The simplest way to cook small fish: have them gutted with heads and tails left on. Season the body cavity and put a bay leaf in each. Add a squeeze of lemon juice and grill for 7–10 minutes, turning once.

Grey Mullet with Tarragon

The fish should be gutted with heads and tails left on. If they are about 350 g/12 oz allow one per person. A larger fish will serve two. Make two or three slashes into each side of the fish. Place in a dish and sprinkle with plenty of chopped fresh tarragon. Pour over a White Wine Marinade (page 76) and leave for at least an hour, preferably two. Drain and grill for

12–20 minutes, depending on the size of the fish. Cook smaller fish at a medium height over the coals, a large fish should be cooked slightly higher. Brush with marinade.

Just before the fish is cooked, strain any remaining marinade into a small saucepan and bring to the boil. Cook for a minute, then remove from the heat and stir in 150 ml/¼ pint single cream and 2 tablespoons snipped chives. Heat very gently and serve with the fish.

Red Mullet in a Vine Leaf Coat

Place a small pat of Garlic Butter (page 29) in the body cavity of each red mullet. Rinse two or three preserved vine leaves for each mullet and blanch them in boiling water for 2 minutes. Drain well. Wrap the mullet tightly in vine leaves, leaving the ends of their heads and their tails free. Place in a fish rack and barbecue high over the coals for 12–15 minutes, turning once.

MUSHROOMS

Button Mushrooms

Skewer these with other vegetables, poultry or fish. Brush with oil before cooking. Alternatively, fill metal skewers with them, brush with melted Garlic Butter (page 29) and grill near the coals for just 1–2 minutes on each side.

Chestnut Mushrooms

These are fairly small and brown, with slightly more flavour than ordinary closed mushrooms. Skewer as above.

Open Mushrooms

Cup mushrooms that are half open or the large, flat mushrooms barbecue quickly over hot coals and they taste excellent. Brush with a little melted butter or oil and cook for 1–2 minutes on each side.

Pork-stuffed Mushrooms

Finely chop 1 small onion and cook it in 25 g/1 oz butter with a crushed clove of garlic for about 10 minutes, stirring occasionally, until soft but not browned. Add seasoning with 350 g/21 oz minced pork and cook until the meat just begins to change colour. Remove from the heat and add 50 g/2 oz breadcrumbs, ½ teaspoon dried sage and ½ teaspoon paprika.

Wipe 8 large cup mushrooms, remove their stalks and brush their tops with a little oil. Chop the stalks and add to the meat mixture. Divide it into eight, then press a portion firmly into each mushroom. Smooth the top and brush with oil, then place meat side down on the barbecue for 3–4 minutes, until browned. Turn carefully and cook the mushrooms for a further 3–4 minutes, then serve.

MUSTARD

I'm a mustard fan and I love discovering new types – with herbs, garlic, mixed with red wine, with horse-radish, Dijon, wholegrain, Swedish (slightly sweeter than other types) and so on. Then there are the dried mustards ready to mix – look out for mustard with apple, for example, which may be soaked in wine, vinegar or even beer and left crunchy or ground to a paste. Look in supermarkets, healthfood shops, gift shops, delicatessens or even wine warehouses to discover different mustards..

Mustard Cream

Finely chop 1 onion and cook it in 25 g/1 oz butter until soft but not browned, about 10–15 minutes, stirring occasionally. Remove from the heat and add 6 tablespoons mild wholegrain mustard. Stir well, then slowly mix in 300 ml/½ pint soured cream or fromage frais. Serve with fish, poultry, meat or vegetables.

Mustard Sauce

Cook a small onion in 25 g/1 oz butter until soft but not browned, stir in 2 tablespoons flour, then slowly add 300 ml/½ pint milk, or half and half milk and stock. Bring to the boil, stirring all the time, and simmer for 2–3 minutes. Remove the pan from the heat and stir in seasoning and mustard to taste. Cover the surface of the sauce with cling film or grease-proof paper to prevent a skin forming and keep warm until ready to serve.

N

NASTURTIUMS

Select and rinse perfect nasturtium flowers and add them to salad leaves and spring onions to make a colourful salad. Larger supermarkets sell the flowers.

Nasturtium leaves have a pleasant peppery taste. Wash and shred them before sprinkling into salads. Add a mixture of flowers and shredded leaves to make a lovely summer's salad – ideal for a festive barbecue.

O

OIL

Oil is brushed over food to keep it moist, to brown it and, in some cases, to crisp it when barbecuing. Oil is used more often than butter as butter tends to burn more readily.

Olive oil gives some foods a lovely flavour, particularly when mixed with herbs and garlic. Sunflower oil is lighter than corn oil. Some of the mixed vegetable oils do not give a good flavour.

Walnut and hazelnut oils are available from some supermarkets and they are delicious in salads. I find that their flavour is somewhat wasted when barbecuing food and they do burn easily, spoiling the flavour of the food. Keep them to mix into salad dressings.

ONIONS

Pickling Onions

Peel and cook on skewers. When cooked with chunks of meat, or other food that takes a while to cook, there is no need to blanch them first. If you want them to grill fairly quickly, then blanch in boiling water for a few minutes and drain well before skewering. Allow about 4–5 minutes, turning once.

Large Onions

Cut large onions into quarters or eighths and skewer instead of pickling onions. Halve and parboil onions, then put them in a rack and grill on the barbecue for 15–20 minutes, brushing with melted butter or oil.

ORANGE

Orange Marinade

Heat the juice of 1 orange with a bay leaf until just boiling. Remove from the heat and add the grated orange rind, 8 crushed green peppercorns, a good pinch each of salt and sugar, and 4 tablespoons sunflower oil.

Caramelized Oranges

Use a vegetable peeler to cut two thin strips of the rind of an orange and cut into fine shreds. Simmer in water until tender – about 5 minutes. Drain. Remove peel and pith off the oranges, allowing one per person. Slice and remove the pips. Arrange the slices in a heatproof dish adding any juices, and top with the orange rind.

Place 225 g/8 oz sugar and 150 ml/ ¼ pint water in a large saucepan and heat gently, stirring until the sugar has dissolved. Stop stirring and bring to the boil. Boil hard until the syrup turns dark golden. Do not leave to cook unattended. Plunge the bottom of the pan into cold water. Pour 2 tablespoons boiling water on to the hot caramel – take great care, protecting your hand with a tea-towel, as the caramel will spit furiously. Stir, then pour over the oranges. Add a little brandy to the oranges if you like. Leave to cool, then chill overnight. Serve with whipped cream.

Fresh Orange Jelly

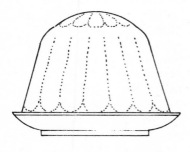

Grate the rind from 2 oranges and mix with the juice from 6 oranges in a saucepan. Add 75 g/3 oz sugar and a cinnamon stick, then heat gently, stirring until the sugar has dissolved and the mixture boils. Remove from the heat, cover and leave until cold. Make the orange juice up to 450 ml/¾ pint with cold water if necessary and remove the cinnamon stick. Add 300 ml/ ½ pint still sweet cider and 300 ml/ ½ pint fromage frais or natural yogurt. In a small basin, sprinkle 25 g/1 oz gelatine over 4 tablespoons cold water and leave for 15 minutes. Set the basin over simmering water and stir until the gelatine has dissolved completely. Stir this into the orange mixture, pour into a wetted 1.15-litre/2-pint mould and chill until set.

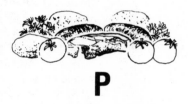

P

PASTA

Cook fresh pasta in plenty of boiling salted water for about 3 minutes, then toss it with lots of butter or olive oil, some chopped parsley or shredded basil and black pepper. Serve grated Parmesan cheese with the pasta.

Dried pasta should be cooked for 15–20 minutes in boiling water, then drained and served as above. Allow 75–100 g/3–4 oz pasta per person. However, if you are serving a pasta salad, or cooked pasta along with a variety of other foods and lots of different barbecued items, 50 g/2 oz per head usually goes a long way. The more people you are feeding and the more dishes you make, the less you need of each one.

<u>Pasta Salad</u>

In a large bowl, mix 2 finely chopped spring onions, 4 tablespoons olive oil, 1 crushed clove of garlic (if you like), 1 deseeded and diced green pepper, 100 g/ 4 oz very lightly cooked French beans (cut in short lengths) and 2 finely sliced celery sticks. Add salt and freshly ground black pepper.

Cook 225 g/8 oz dried pasta shapes in boiling salted water for 15–20 minutes, until just tender. Drain and put straight into the bowl, tossing the pasta with the other ingredients. Cover and leave to cool. Before serving, add 150 ml/ ¼ pint soured cream or fromage frais and 2 tablespoons lemon juice. Shred all the leaves from about 6 large sprigs of basil and toss them into the salad with some chopped parsley. Serves four.

PEANUTS

In Dressing

Mix 2 tablespoons crunchy peanut butter with 4 tablespoons oil and 4 tablespoons cider vinegar. Add salt, pepper, some chopped parsley and a crushed clove of garlic if you like. Whisk well to make a delicious salad dressing – good on Coleslaw (page 42), with lightly cooked cauliflower mixed with spring onions, or with Potato Salad (page 96).

In Salad

Roughly chop salted peanuts or unsalted roasted peanuts and toss them into Rice Salad (page 101), with a crunchy green salad that has lots of chopped celery in it, or with Tomato and Orange Salad (page 102).

PEARS

Peel, core and quarter ripe pears. Place 4 quarters on a large square of foil, top with 2 tablespoons orange juice and 2 teaspoons clear honey. Add a few toasted flaked almonds and close the package. Heat on the barbecue for about 5 minutes, slightly longer over dying coals.

Pear and Walnut Salad

Peel, core and dice 4 ripe but firm pears. Toss with the leaves from a bunch of watercress and place on a shallow bed of shredded lettuce heart. Mix a dressing of 3 tablespoons mayonnaise, 3 tablespoons natural yogurt, 2 tablespoons orange juice, salt and freshly ground black pepper and a little grated nutmeg to taste. Spoon this over the pears and top with 50 g/ 2 oz roughly chopped walnuts. Toss the salad just before it is eaten.

PEPPERS

Look out for red, yellow, orange or even purple and white peppers.

Brush with a little oil. Roast them whole at a medium height over the barbecue until they just begin to blister, turning frequently until the flesh is soft – about 15–20 minutes. To serve, put them on a plate and use a sharp knife to cut out the stalk end, taking with it all the seeds – hold on to the stalk as you do this. Halve the pepper, scrape away the remaining seeds and serve topped with a dip (page 45), with a savoury butter (page 28) or lemon juice.

Pepper Salad

Barbecue whole peppers near the coals until their skin is blistered all over. Scrape the skin off under cold water, then cut out the stalk and remove seeds. Halve the peppers, cut into strips, season and dress with olive oil and a little lemon juice.

PICKLES

Gherkins, pickled onions and pickled red cabbage all go well with hamburgers and sausages. Try pickling peaches or apples as a deliciously unusual accompaniment to pork or gammon.

Sweetened Spiced Vinegar

Heat 1.15 litres/2 pints white vinegar with a dried red chilli, 1 tablespoon whole coriander, 6 black peppercorns, 1 cinnamon stick, a blade of mace, 1 tablespoon allspice and a slice of onion. Heat the mixture very gently, with the lid on the pan, until it is just simmering. Turn off the heat and leave until cold. Strain the vinegar through scalded muslin or a fine sieve. Pour it into a clean pan and add 225 g/8 oz sugar. Stir over low heat until dissolved. Cool.

Pickled Apples

Peel, core and quarter well-flavoured eating apples. Pack into jars and top up with sweetened spiced vinegar. Shake out all bubbles, cover tightly and store for at least 2 weeks before serving. Apples are also good mixed with pickling onions.

Pickled Peaches

Place perfect, firm, ripe peaches in a bowl and cover with freshly boiling water. Leave for about a minute, drain and peel. Halve and remove the stones, then pack the peaches in jars and top up with sweetened spiced vinegar. Shake out all bubbles, cover and store for at least 2 weeks before serving.

PINEAPPLE

Pineapple combines well with pork, sausages and meat. For juicy, full-flavoured (and inexpensive) kebabs, skewer chunks of smoked Dutch sausage (look out for the one with garlic added) with small pickling onions, chunks of pepper and chunks of drained canned pineapple. Brush with oil and grill for about 5 minutes on each side until the sausage is sizzling. If you like, forget about the onions and peppers and just have sausage and pineapple – it is good with baked potatoes.

Skewer chunks of fresh or canned pineapple, brush with melted butter and dip in soft brown sugar. Caramelize the coating near the coals for 1–2 minutes on each side.

Pineapple Rum Packets

Peel and halve a fresh pineapple. Remove the core and all the spines on the outside. Slice and divide between squares of foil. A small pineapple will serve four. Sprinkle each portion with 1–2 tablespoons rum and 1–2 tablespoons soft brown sugar. Close the foil tightly around the fruit and heat on the barbecue for 3–5 minutes, longer if the coals are dying. Serve with whipped cream and top with crushed meringues or Amaretti biscuits.

PLAICE

Plaice fillets may be rolled and barbecued but handle carefully to avoid breaking the fish as you turn the rolls. Barbecued whole plaice is better.

Plaice Rolls

Skin and halve 4 plaice fillets. Put the skinned side down and sprinkle the fish with the grated rind of 1 lemon, 2 tablespoons chopped fresh dill (or a little dried dill), salt, freshly ground black pepper and a squeeze of lemon juice. Roll up from the wide end and thread on to metal skewers. Brush with oil and cook for about 5 minutes on each side, turning carefully with a metal slice.

Whole Plaice

These are sold ready gutted. Rinse and dry the fish. Brush with oil and barbecue at a medium height over the coals for about 10 minutes (for a 450 g/1 lb fish), turning once. The best way to turn the fish is with two slices, loosening the tail, head and edges first. Enclosing the fish in a cooking rack makes this easy. Serve at once, with lemon wedges and black pepper.

PLANNING

It doesn't matter what are you are planning, make a list – or several. The following is a quick run through of things to sort out and remember.

★ *PEOPLE* How many? How old? Eating habits? Sort out numbers and whether there are food restrictions, for example are you planning a vegetarian meal or a mixed meal? If you are inviting children, make sure they are catered for in terms of entertainment and safety as well as food. So, list the people, including the number of children and you are ready to plan the next stage.

★ *COOKING ARRANGEMENTS* Once you know how many you can evaluate the catering problems. A couple of years ago, on holiday, we met a hotel manager who cringed as I muttered about barbecues: he related the nightmare of a wedding reception at which the bride and groom wanted a barbecue. The marquee was set, the vast grill and fire was laid out and the guests arrived, downed the welcome drink and looked for the food. The barbecue was a disaster – the charcoal took its usual time to heat, the food had to be cooked, the guests were starving . . .

You may not be catering for a hundred but even if there are just four, do plan ahead. What are you cooking on ? Do you have a gas or electric barbecue or do you have enough charcoal? Remember the lighters or kindling. Is the barbecue big enough for the food to be cooked?

Have the barbecue conveniently near the kitchen, in a safe place, with a table to hand. If there is a chance of rain, can a waterproof cover be erected safely? Basic waterproof awnings are quite inexpensive and they are a good buy.

Plan the time you expect guests to arrive and note the time you ought to light the barbecue, allowing it to heat up and giving time to cook all the food (particularly important if you are cooking a joint of meat).

★ *FOOD/MENU* Plan the menu: have dips or nibbles to serve while the main course is cooking. Decide on the main food to barbecue, either one item or a selection of foods. You may like to barbecue snacks for a first course. Once you have decided on the barbecued food, think about accompaniments – bread, potatoes, salads, sauces and relishes. Then pudding: barbecued fruit, a make-ahead dessert or a bowl of exotic fruit. Be totally practical and decide on a menu you can prepare with ease.

When thinking about quantities to allow, err on the generous side. Remember that fresh air is a great appetite booster and guests are usually willing to try a variety of barbecued food.

★ *DRINKS* Wine, cider, beer, a punch, plus non-alcoholic drinks such as alcohol-free wine, fruit juices, mineral water and something for children. If you are planning a fairly large gathering, ask guests to bring a contribution – a bottle of wine or some non-alcoholic offering. Reduced-alcohol wines, beers and ciders are a good idea but make sure drivers realize they are reduced-alcohol, not alcohol-free.

★ *CROCKERY AND CUTLERY* If you are planning a large gathering, think about disposable plates and paper napkins, even disposable 'glasses'. Plastic cups are a good idea for small children. Alternatively, ask a friend to bring a few plates, knives and forks. For a 'formal' barbecue, look in local directories for catering suppliers who hire out crockery. If you buy a case of wine, many big suppliers offer glasses on loan for free or for a small charge (you have to pay for breakages). If you entertain regularly, it is a good idea to buy cheap, plain glasses in sales and store them in a box in the attic.

★ *SHOPPING AND COOKING* Make a detailed shopping list. List the cooking order. Make any desserts or dishes that can be prepared in advance the day before and chill. Put food to marinate if necessary. Think through all the following cooking notes and jot them down on your list so that you know what to do and when.

Wash salad ingredients and soak celery, fennel or spring onions in iced water several hours in advance. Have baking potatoes scrubbed and cook any food that must be taken to a cooked stage before barbecuing, for example new potatoes. If you are cooking for a crowd, and plan to serve chicken, cook portions just before you intend to barbecue or even the day before, in which case they should be cooled and chilled. Prepare meat and vegetables for kebabs, but assemble just before barbecuing. Make pasta and rice salads earlier in the day and prepare any fruit that you want to barbecue.

PLUMS

Skewer halved and stoned plums with other fruit (see page 53).

Quick Plum Sauce

Sieve 175g/6 oz plum jam (or damson jam) and mix in 3 tablespoons cider vinegar. Add a crushed clove of garlic. Brush this over boneless duck breasts or duck portions towards the end of cooking. Also good with pork.

PORK

Always make sure that the meat is cooked through before serving. Check by piercing the thickest part with the point of a knife and continue to cook if there is any sign of uncooked meat or blood. The following is a guide to cooking times, placing the meat at a medium height over the coals and turning often.

Sparerib Chops – *20–25 minutes*
Spareribs – *15–20 minutes (see below)*
Loin Chops – *20–25 minutes*
Cubes on Kebabs – *25–30 minutes*

Honey Spareribs

Separate 1 kg/2¼ lb meaty spareribs and trim off any excess fat. Simmer in enough stock to cover for 20 minutes, drain and place in a dish. Mix 2 tablespoons honey, 3 tablespoons soy sauce and 1 crushed clove of garlic. Brush this all over the ribs and leave until cold, then chill for several hours. Grill at a medium height over the coals for 15 minutes, turning often until browned and crisp. Simmering the meat first gives the most tender results.

Spiced Chops

Make horizontal slits into 4 loin chops and slip bay leaves into them. Brush with a little oil, sprinkle with seasoning and 1 tablespoon ground mace. Leave to marinate for at least an hour, then barbecue for 20–25 minutes, turning once.

Ginger Kebabs

Place 450 g/1 lb lean pork cubes in a basin. Add 1 teaspoon ground ginger, salt and freshly ground black pepper, the grated rind of 1 orange, 2 tablespoons orange juice and 2 tablespoons oil. Mix well, leave to marinate for at least an hour, preferably overnight. Thread on to metal skewers with 1 large green pepper, deseeded and cut in chunks, and a drained 225-g/8-oz can of pineapple chunks. Barbecue for 25–30 minutes, turning often and brushing with marinade.

POTATOES

Scrub, prick and bake potatoes in the oven for about 1¼–1½ hours at 190°C/375°F/gas 5, until tender. If you like, wrap them in foil while they cook in the conventional oven, then brown and crisp their skins on the barbecue.

Cook scrubbed new potatoes in boiling water for about 10–15 minutes, until tender. Drain and thread on to metal skewers. Brush with melted butter and brown at a medium height over the coals, about 5 minutes on each side.

▶ Three-quarters cook large potatoes in their skins, either by baking or boiling, or use the microwave for speed. Brush with oil and finish cooking on the barbecue rack.

Potato Salad

Boil 4 medium potatoes in their skins for about 20 minutes, until tender. Drain and rinse under cold water, then peel and cut into cubes. Place in a bowl and sprinkle with 4 tablespoons snipped chives. Cover and cool. Mix 150 ml/¼ pint mayonnaise with 2 tablespoons single cream, natural yogurt or fromage frais and seasoning. Pour this over the salad and mix lightly before serving.

PRAWNS

Mediterranean Prawns

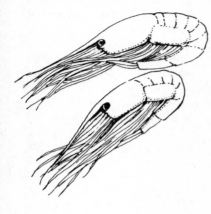

Good fishmongers sell frozen, peeled, uncooked Mediterranean prawns (or King prawns). These are delicious skewered and grilled. For best results, allow them to part thaw before threading on to skewers, brushing with melted butter and cooking at a medium height over the coals until the flesh turns from opaque to white with tinges of pink. Turn once or twice and brush with melted butter during cooking. They may be marinated in garlic and oil, with spices such as coriander (ground or chopped leaves) or ginger (ground or grated fresh root), before cooking. Grated lemon rind and juice may also be added.

Prawn Parcels

Blanch 8 large Iceberg lettuce leaves in boiling water for a few seconds to soften them. Drain well and dry on absorbent kitchen paper.

Mix 225 g/8 oz peeled cooked prawns (thawed if frozen and patted dry), 2 finely chopped spring onions and seasoning to taste. Melt 25 g/1 oz butter and add 2 teaspoons ground coriander. Stir over the heat for 2 minutes, then pour this mixture over the prawns and mix well.

Divide the prawns between the

lettuce leaves and fold the leaves around them to make neat parcels. Brush with melted butter or oil and place in a cooking rack. Barbecue for 2–3 minutes on each side to heat through, then serve at once.

Prawn Balls

Thaw 450 g/1 lb peeled cooked prawns. Drain well and mince (a food processor or liquidizer may be used). Mix with 1 egg white, salt and freshly ground black pepper, 1 teaspoon grated lemon rind, 25 g/1 oz fresh white breadcrumbs, 2 tablespoons chopped parsley or coriander leaves and a squeeze of lemon juice. Shape into walnut-sized balls and thread on to four metal skewers, pressing the mixture on the skewers. Brush with oil and grill fairly near the coals for 3 minutes on each side until lightly browned and firm. Serve with lemon wedges.

PRUNES

Buy ready-to-eat prunes and wrap them in halved rindless bacon rashers. Thread on to skewers and grill for about 5 minutes on each side, until the bacon is browned. Serve with drinks.

R

RABBIT

Farmed rabbit is tender and it cooks quickly. Super-markets sell rabbit joints and butchers often have prepared rabbit. Chinese rabbit is particularly good, very lean and tender, with a nice flavour. If there is any fat on the meat, trim it all off before marinating as it has an unpleasant taste.

The portions should be fairly small and first brushed with oil or marinade, seasoned, then cooked at a medium height above the coals for 20–25 minutes, until lightly browned and cooked through.

Heat remaining marinade to serve with the rabbit. Mustard Cream (page 81), Mustard Sauce (page 81) or savoury butters go well (page 28).

RADISH

For a slightly exotic salad, peel and coarsely grate a large white radish (mooli or daikon), toss it with lemon juice and a little oil, adding seasoning to taste. Pile on a bed of shredded Chinese leaves and serve at once.

RHUBARB

Trim fresh young rhubarb and slice. Place a small pile on a square of foil, sprinkle with a little orange juice and honey or sugar, then close the foil tightly and cook the rhubarb on the barbecue for about 10 minutes, until softened. Chopped preserved ginger and syrup from the jar may be used instead of the orange juice and honey.

RICE

Serve rice either hot or cold in salad as an accompaniment instead of bread or potatoes. Place 225 g/8 oz long-grain rice in a pan with 600 ml/1 pint water and a little salt. Bring to the boil, cover and reduce the heat, then simmer gently for about 15–20 minutes, until the rice has absorbed all the water. Fork in a knob of butter and some chopped parsley to serve. Try the following flavourings:

★ *LEMON* Add the grated rind of 1 lemon to the rice 5 minutes before the end of cooking. Good with fish.

★ *HERB* Add 2 tablespoons freshly chopped mixed fresh herbs to the cooked rice.

★ *TOMATO* Add 4 peeled, deseeded and chopped tomatoes to the cooked rice with the parsley.

Basmati Rice

Indian rice with a lovely scent and delicious flavour. Wash the grains carefully in cold water, swooshing them with your fingers, then drain before cooking as above. If you like, add a cinnamon stick, 2 green cardamoms and a bay leaf to the cooking water, and top the cooked rice with onion slices, fried in butter until golden.

Rice Salad

Cook the rice as above. Meanwhile, mix 4 tablespoons olive oil and 2 tablespoons lemon juice with salt and freshly ground black pepper in a bowl. Add 2 chopped spring onions and the freshly cooked rice. Toss well. Cover and leave to cool. Other vegetables may be added to the cooled rice: try chopped celery, some cooked peas, finely sliced button mushrooms, diced red pepper and cooked sweet corn.

S

SAFETY

★ **SET** the barbecue in a safe place, sheltered from fierce wind and away from any petrol cans or similar inflammable materials.
★ **NEVER** use petrol or paraffin to light a barbecue.
★ **NEVER** turn on a gas barbecue with the lid closed before lighting.
★ **KEEP** children at a safe distance from the barbecue. Always supervise youngsters.
★ **NEVER** leave the barbecue unattended.
★ **HAVE** long-handled utensils and fire tongs near. Protect hands and forearms with oven mitts.
★ **KEEP** a water spray (plant spray) at hand to douse flames caused by fat dripping on charcoal. Never spray gas or electric barbecues.

SALADS

Essential to complement barbecued food. Look out for the following salad leaves:

* ★ *LOLLO ROSSO* Slightly frilly and tinged with dark red, they taste like a lettuce. They are not bitter.
* ★ *ENDIVE* Large, frilly, slightly spiky leaves with a firm texture. Easy to grow and adds texture to a salad.
* ★ *RADICCHIO* Small round heads of red chicory with a bitter flavour to add texture, colour and a contrast in flavour.
* ★ *CHICORY* Oval heads, with pale green to white crunchy leaves. Shred them before adding to a salad.
* ★ *ICEBERG LETTUCE* This has a good flavour and excellent crunchy texture.
* ★ *LAMB'S LETTUCE* Small dark leaves, a bit like miniature spinach.

Mix as many leaves as you can find, or would like, to make a good mixed salad.

Tomato and Orange Salad

Peel and slice 450 g/1 lb tomatoes. Peel and remove all pith from 3 oranges, catching the juice. Over a basin, cut between the membranes and remove all the fruit segments. Arrange the tomato slices and orange segments on a platter. Mix about 2 tablespoons light salad oil with the orange juice and freshly ground black pepper, then pour this over the salad. Serve sprinkled with snipped chives.

Salad Dressings

Decide on a basic oil and vinegar dressing that you particularly like.

I use one-third vinegar to oil (sometimes slightly less if I want just a hint of tartness), adding equal proportions of salt and sugar, a good grind of freshly ground black pepper and a dollop of Dijon or wholegrain mustard. This basic dressing may be varied by adding a clove of garlic, herbs or citrus rinds.

For a light yogurt dressing, season natural yogurt and mix in some chopped parsley, snipped chives and a little grated nutmeg, if you like.

SALMON

Salmon, either whole or in steaks is superb barbecued. Brush them with butter and cook for about 5 minutes on each side, until firm, bright and marked with the lines of the cooking rack. Serve topped with a little dill and lemon wedges.

Spice up salmon steaks with a little freshly crushed coriander and some grated lemon rind, but do not overdo the flavouring ingredients with salmon.

To barbecue a whole salmon, have it gutted with head and tail left on, and descaled. Place bay leaves and parsley sprigs in the body cavity, then brush very lightly with oil. Wrap two thick bands of cooking foil around a large fish, one near the head end and the other near the tail. Twist the ends of the foil to secure the bands firmly in place, then use them to help turn the fish over during cooking. Cook the salmon high above the heat until well browned. Use two large fish slices to turn the salmon;

cooking the second side until well browned. The cooking time depends on the thickness: test the fish by piercing the middle of the back with the point of a sharp knife. The mark will not show if you take care and you should be able to see whether this thickest part of the fish is cooked. As a guide, a 3.4 kg/7½ lb salmon takes 20–30 minutes. Very large fish may be enclosed in foil and allowed to cook slowly.

SANGRIA

Pour a bottle of Spanish red wine into a bowl. Add a sliced orange and lemon, a cored, quartered and sliced eating apple and lots of ice. Dissolve 75 g/3 oz sugar in 150 ml/¼ pint water, pour into the wine and top up with 600 ml/1 pint sparkling mineral water. Add plenty of ice and stand for 15 minutes before serving.

SARDINES

Cook whole or gutted with heads and tails left on. Brush with olive oil and season all over, then place in a cooking rack and grill fairly near the coals until blistered. Turn and cook the second side, then serve with wedges of lemon and plenty of fresh crusty bread. They take about 2–3 minutes on each side. (Look out for frozen sardines – they are quite good.)

SATAY

Satay, an Indonesian speciality, consists of small cubes of meat (about 1.5 cm/¾ in or less) skewered and grilled, served with a spicy peanut sauce.

Mix 450 g/1 lb cubed meat with 1 tablespoon ground coriander, 1 teaspoon ground ginger, salt and freshly ground black pepper and a little groundnut oil (or other oil). Cover and leave to marinate for several hours, preferably overnight.

For the satay sauce, cook 1 finely chopped onion in 2 tablespoons groundnut oil (or other) with 2 crushed cloves of garlic until very soft. Do this over a low heat for about 15 minutes. Add 75 g/3 oz salted peanuts, ¼–½ teaspoon chilli powder, the juice of ½ lemon, 1 tablespoon soft brown sugar, 1 tablespoon soy sauce and 150 ml/ ¼ pint water. Heat gently, stirring, until simmering, then cook for a couple of minutes. Cool slightly and liquidize until smooth.

Skewer the meat and cook at a medium height over the coals, allowing about 10 minutes for beef or lamb, slightly longer for pork and chicken for safety. Brush with any juices during cooking and turn once or twice. Serve with peanut sauce.

SAUSAGES

Good sausages, cooked high above the barbecue until golden and crisp, are delicious. There are lots of different types of British sausage and good supermarkets provide a choice. To a certain extent you get what you pay for and economy sausages are not particularly exciting. Local butchers often make their own sausages and these can be very good; for example, my butcher makes thick pork sausages, delicious chipolatas (thin pork sausages), pork and beef sausages, spicy sausages and extra long sausages. They do not contain preservative so are sold freshly made or frozen.

★ *CUMBERLAND* A long, curled sausage, seasoned with spices and having a coarse texture. Cook it curled on the barbecue (secure it with a skewer), then cut it into 'slices' when cooked.

★ *OXFORD* These are made from veal, pork and beef.

★ *LINCOLNSHIRE* Seasoned with sage.

★ *COTSWOLD* Seasoned with sage and thyme.

★ *LONDON* Traditionally a mild sausage, flavoured with ginger or nutmeg.

★ *OTHER TYPES* There are also low-fat sausages, skinless sausages and small cocktail sausages for threading on skewers (good with kidneys).

In addition to traditional varieties, venison sausages are now increasingly available and duck sausages may be purchased from specialist shops (or through mail order suppliers). Both types are dark, rich and quite dry; good with a marinade or sauce.

★ *CONTINENTAL SAUSAGES* If you have an Italian food shop nearby, they may sell full-flavoured fresh cotechino – delicious poached until cooked, then barbecued until golden. A famous French speciality is Toulouse sausage, meaty and spicy, good poached and then barbecued.

★ *HOMEMADE SAUSAGES* If you enjoy new food discoveries, have a go at making your own sausages – it is not too difficult. Casings are available from small butchers, although you may have to buy many yards more than you will fill in one go. They are salted and will keep in a sealed container in the refrigerator for two or three months.

★ *COOKING TIME* About 20 minutes, turning often. Chipolatas cook in 12–15 minutes. Curled sausages take slightly longer.

Pork Sausages

Ask your butcher to mince 450 g/ 1 lb pork twice or do this at home. Mix 75 g/3 oz fresh breadcrumbs, ½ teaspoon ground mace, ½ teaspoon dried sage, ½ teaspoon ground coriander, ½ teaspoon dried thyme and salt and pepper into the meat. Moisten the mixture with water – about 4–6 tablespoons.

Wine and Garlic Sausages

Use half and half minced pork and beef (braising steak minced two or three times), making 450 g/1 lb in all. Finely chop 225 g/8 oz rindless streaky bacon and mix it with the meat. Add 2 crushed cloves of garlic, 1 teaspoon ground mace, 10 crushed juniper berries and 150 ml/¼ pint red wine. Mix well, cover and leave to marinate for at least 2 hours. Season, add 2 tablespoons chopped parsley and 75 g/ 3 oz fresh breadcrumbs. Mix well.

Filling Skins

Soak the skins for 30 minutes, drain, rinse and put in clean water. You will need a large piping bag fitted with a large plain nozzle. Have the nozzle protruding from the bag as far as possible. Fill the bag with your sausage mixture. Push a length of soaked skin on to the nozzle; when you have pushed on as much as you can, cut the other end and tie a knot in it. Hold the bag firmly in one hand, resting it on the work surface for support, and squeeze the meat into the skins. Use your other hand to regulate the amount of skin coming off the end of the nozzle. The sausage must be plump but not tightly filled. When the meat or skin is finished, tie a knot in the end and cut off any remaining skin. Curl the sausage or twist it into individual sausages. Do not prick natural skins before cooking.

★ *FREEZING* Homemade sausages freeze well but a word of warning: I made a large batch of strong garlic sausages (4 cloves instead of 2), with lots of herbs and I froze a good number. Wrapped in two layers of heavy polythene bags they still infused the contents of one corner of my freezer with garlic! Allow sausages to thaw before cooking.

Sausage Burgers

Mix 450 g/1 lb sausagemeat, 100 g/4 oz chopped mushrooms, 25 g/1 oz fresh breadcrumbs, a pinch each of dried thyme and sage, salt and freshly ground black pepper and a crushed clove of garlic (optional). Shape into eight small round burgers, brush with a little oil and barbecue for 3–4 minutes on each side, until golden and cooked through.

SAVELOYS

If you like them, they are good barbecued and they cook quickly, about 8 minutes, until darkened and sizzling. Turn often.

SCALLOPS

On Shells

Place one large cleaned scallop on each shell. Sprinkle with a little freshly ground pepper and a squeeze of lemon juice. Top with a sprig of fennel or dill and cover with foil. Cook for 5–7 minutes at a medium height above the coals (higher if very hot). After 5 minutes they will still be soft and juicy in the middle, cooked through after 7 minutes. These are delicious with crusty bread.

Scallop Brochettes

Buy large scallops and cut them in half. Wrap each piece of scallop in half a rasher of rindless bacon (stretch the rashers with the back of a knife if necessary) and thread on to skewers. Grill for 8–10 minutes, turning once or twice, until the bacon is cooked and browned.

SHARK

Shark is a firm, dry, meaty fish, usually sold in steaks. Marinate the fish in oil and lemon juice (half and half), adding a bay leaf or two, some chopped parsley, 1 tablespoon chopped spring onion and some seasoning. Cook the steaks for 8–10 minutes, turning often and brushing with marinade. Serve topped with Lemon Butter (page 29).

★ **SEASONINGS** Try marinating shark in oil and lemon with a small chopped clove of garlic, a sprinkling of ground coriander and some freshly grated nutmeg. Alternatively, combine finely chopped fresh root ginger, lemon or lime juice and grated rind, and chopped spring onions. Add a little oil and seasoning.

SKEWERS

Metal skewers are best for barbecuing. I have used fine wooden or bamboo skewers but they tend to smoulder even if they do not catch fire. I once used metal skewers with wooden ends and the ends burnt.

As well as skewering small pieces of food, use skewers to keep food in shape, for example joints of meat.

SMOKED DUTCH SAUSAGE

This is ready cooked, so it barbecues quickly. Look out for the variety with added garlic. Cook the curved sausage whole, until browned and sizzling on one side (about 4–5 minutes), turn and cook the second side, then cut in chunks to serve. Alternatively, cut into chunks and skewer with vegetables.

SMOKING

Hickory chips or packets of herb, spice and wood mixtures are available. Follow the manufacturer's instructions, usually wetting or soaking the smoking material. Place straight on the charcoal, or in a pierced foil container on a gas barbecue. A covered barbecue gives best results but the flavour is imparted to some extent on an open grill. Chicken, turkey breast and trout are all delicious cooked over smoke. Try also smoking leg of lamb or salmon steaks.

SPICES

Ginger and Lemon Marinade

Lightly peel and grate 25 g/1 oz fresh root ginger. Mix it with the grated rind of 1 lemon and the juice of ½ lemon. Add seasoning and 4 tablespoons oil, with a crushed clove of garlic if liked.

Coriander and Cumin Marinade

Mix 2 tablespoons ground coriander, 1 tablespoon ground cumin, ¼ teaspoon turmeric, 2 tablespoons grated onion, 4 tablespoons oil, 2 tablespoons lemon juice or natural yogurt, and seasoning.

Mace and Orange Marinade

Mix 1 teaspoon ground mace, the grated rind of ½ orange and the juice of 1 orange. Add 4 tablespoons oil, salt and pepper.

SPIT-ROASTING

Battery-powered spits may be used on many types of barbecue. Good for joints or whole poultry and particularly successful with lidded barbecues. Allow about 10–15 minutes per 450 g/1 lb plus 10 minutes for beef; 15–20 minutes per 450 g/1 lb plus 15–20 minutes for lamb; 25 minutes per 450 g/1 lb plus 25 minutes for pork. These times are a guide; the shape and thickness of the joint is also important.

Meat should be boned, marinated, and skewered on the spit in a neat shape. Baste often during cooking and check for doneness by piercing the thick part of the joint with a knife.

SQUID

These were very much an experiment and they turned out to be a delicious surprise.

Stuffed Squid

Clean 8 squid: pull out the head and tentacles in one piece, then pull out and discard the plastic-like quill. Rinse well and rub off the dark, spotted skin to leave a clean, white pouch. Drain on absorbent kitchen paper. Cut off the tentacles and discard the rest. Wash the tentacles well, then chop them finely.

Cook a finely chopped small onion and 1 large crushed clove of garlic in 2 tablespoons olive oil until tender but not browned. Add the chopped tentacles, 2 large peeled, deseeded and chopped tomatoes and a little salt and freshly ground black pepper. Cover and simmer the mixture for 5 minutes. Remove from the heat, add 50 g/2 oz fresh breadcrumbs and 16 shredded fresh basil leaves. Check the seasoning, add a squeeze of lemon juice and spoon this mixture into the prepared squid, leaving enough room for the ends to be closed on skewers.

Thread 2 stuffed squid on to a metal skewer, pushing it through the open end and just above the point at the other end. Do not lift the squid by the skewer alone or the flesh may rip. Place on a plate and brush with oil, then cook for about 10 minutes, turning once, until golden all over. The stuffing swells during cooking, so spoon away any that begins to escape. Serve immediately with wedges of lemon.

STRAWBERRIES

One of the simplest summer desserts. Hull ripe strawberries, place them in a dish and sprinkle with a little orange liqueur. Leave to macerate for a couple of hours, stirring once or twice, then serve with whipped cream.

SWEET POTATO

Peel off the red skin and cut the sweet potato into thick slices. Simmer in salted water for 15 minutes or until tender. Brush with melted butter and sprinkle with just a little ground cinnamon, if liked, then barbecue for about 5 minutes on each side, until browned and slightly crisp. Good as an accompaniment for spicy sausages, with bacon rolls or with pork chops.

SWORDFISH

A firm, meaty fish which barbecues well. Marinate it with oil before cooking and baste it often. Cooking time depends on thickness. Small steaks serve one, large steaks may be cut into portions when cooked. Try this tasty marinade.

Mix the grated rind and juice of 1 lime or orange with 2 table-spoons chopped capers and 4 tablespoons oil. Add salt and pepper and pour over 4 small swordfish steaks or 2 large ones. Leave for 2–3 hours, then barbecue at a medium height over the coals, brushing with marinade, for about 10 minutes, turning once. The fish should be nicely browned outside and cooked through.

T

TARAMASALATA

Remove the skin from 350 g/ 12 oz smoked cod's roe. Place the roe in a food processor with 1 tablespoon grated onion. Squeeze the juice from ½ lemon and add a little to the roe. Measure 100 ml/

4 fl oz olive oil and add about 1 tablespoon to the roe. Process until smooth. Scrape the mixture into the middle of the bowl, then slowly pour the remaining oil into the bowl as the mixture is processed to form a creamy liaison. If any of the oil is not readily absorbed, do not add any more but scrape the mixture into the middle of the bowl and process for a few seconds, then see if the mixture will take up more oil. Gradually stir in seasoning and lemon juice to taste. Chill lightly before serving.

TOMATOES

Cut a cross in the top of the fruit, brush with a little oil and grill for about 3–4 minutes. If the barbecue is very hot the tomatoes will soften very quickly. Do not allow them to become squashy and unpleasant. Turn once during cooking.

Skewer small whole or halved medium tomatoes with other foods, on kebabs. Mix them with ingredients that cook quickly otherwise the tomatoes will be very mushy before the main food is cooked.

Tomato Sauce

Cook 1 finely chopped onion and a chopped clove of garlic in 2 tablespoons olive oil until the onion is soft but not browned. Add a bay leaf, 1 kg/2¼ lb chopped tomatoes, 4 tablespoons stock, 1 tablespoon sugar, salt and pepper. Cover and simmer gently for 40 minutes. Discard the bay leaf, liquidize and sieve the sauce, then reheat it gently, tasting for seasoning. Serve with barbecued fish, poultry, meat or vegetables. If the sauce is for vegetarians use a vegetable stock.

Basil Tomato Concassé

Peel, deseed and chop 450 g/1 lb ripe tomatoes. Sprinkle with 1 teaspoon caster sugar, salt and freshly ground black pepper. Add 1 tablespoon very finely chopped spring onion and gradually stir in 3 tablespoons olive oil, pounding or mashing the tomatoes so that they mix well with the oil. Sprinkle with a little finely shredded fresh basil and allow to stand, covered, for an hour. Stir well and taste for seasoning before serving. This is particularly good with fish, chicken or turkey.

TONGS

Buy good quality, long-handled tongs. I have a hinged pair (like huge scissors) and find them far better than those from one piece of curved metal.

As well as tongs for turning the food, you will need a pair of fire tongs for handling hot charcoal.

TUNA

Fresh tuna is dark and dry. It is usually sold in large steaks, but some supermarkets intend to offer this fish in smaller portions to be called 'loins'.

Marinate the tuna in oil and herbs before cooking. Olive oil with chopped fresh or dried marjoram and a little lemon rind is ideal. Flavour 6 tablespoons oil with 1 tablespoon chopped fresh marjoram or 1 teaspoon dried. Add 1 teaspoon grated lemon rind and seasoning. Spoon over the fish, cover and chill for 2 hours or longer.

Cook at a medium height over the coals, brushing often with marinade, for about 5–7 minutes on each side, until browned and cooked through.

TURKEY

Buy breast fillets for barbecuing. Cut them into thin slices and dust with seasoned flour. Add a sprinkling of paprika if you like – it gives the turkey a pleasantly mild, peppery flavour. Barbecue for about 8–10 minutes, turning often and brushing with a little melted butter once the flour coating has set and browned slightly. Serve with soured cream and chives.

Turkey Kebabs

I made these when I was trying to cut down on the calories recently. Cut 450 g/1 lb turkey breast into small cubes. Place in a bowl with 150 ml/¼ pint fromage frais, the grated rind of ½ lemon and 1 teaspoon finely chopped fresh rosemary. Add a little seasoning and mix well to coat all the pieces. Cover and chill for at least 2 hours. Thread on to metal skewers and cook over the barbecue for about 20 minutes, turning often and brushing with marinade, until well browned and cooked through. Serve with chunks of crisp Iceberg lettuce, slivers of spring onion and thinly sliced cucumber. Fluffy baked potatoes go very well.

U

UTENSILS

▶ **Long-handled Tongs** For turning and removing food.
Cooking Racks To enclose even pieces of food that break easily, for example fish. Large or small, from cook shops as well as barbecue supplliers.
Fire Tongs For moving hot coals, or adding extra coal.
Enormous Forks For lifting and turning joints.
Oven Mitts For protecting hands and forearms.
Apron It can be a dirty business!
Water Spray A plant spray to deal with flare-ups.

V

VEAL

Barbecue tender cuts, such as chops or escalopes.

Veal Chops with Sage

Snip 2 fresh sage leaves into fine shreds and sprinkle over each chop. Season with salt and freshly ground black pepper and drizzle over 2 teaspoons sunflower oil. Leave to marinate, covered, for several hours. Allow 1 chop per serving. Barbecue at a medium height over the coals, brushing with the oil and sage, for 20 minutes, turning once, until golden and cooked through. Serve with Tomato Sauce (page 115).

Escalopes with Mozzarella

Beat 4 veal escalopes until quite thin (do this between sheets of greaseproof paper). Mix 3 tablespoons olive oil with 1 teaspoon tomato purée, a squeeze of lemon juice, salt and freshly ground black pepper. Brush this over the pieces of veal and cook them fairly near the coals until well browned on one side – about 4 minutes. Turn and top the cooked side of each escalope with 2 slices of mozzarella cheese. Cook for a further 4 minutes, until the second side of the meat is well browned and the mozzarella has melted. Use a slice to transfer the veal to serving plates. Top each with a little shredded fresh basil and a peeled and chopped tomato.

VEGETABLE KEBABS

Prepare chunks of aubergine (salted, page 21), slices of courgette, diced peppers, mushrooms, canned or cooked baby corn, cooked new potatoes (in skins), Jerusalem artichokes (in skins) and chunks of lightly cooked parsnip. Marinate with oil and freshly chopped mixed herbs, then skewer nd barbecue, turning often, for about 15 minutes.

VINE LEAVES

Buy these fresh, in packets or canned. Before use drain preserved leaves and rinse. Wash fresh leaves. Blanch in boiling water until just tender – about 3 minutes. Drain and pat dry on absorbent kitchen paper. Wrap around delicate foods before barbecuing. They help to keep the food moist and flavoursome during cooking, and at the same time impart their own flavour to it. Fish, such as trout, cheese (particularly tangy goat's cheese) and other ingredients which require little cooking may be enclosed in vine leaves. The leaves should be brushed with oil and cooked until they are browned, but not burnt, on the outside.

Stuffed Vine Leaves

Cook 100 g/4 oz long-grain rice in plenty of boiling water for 10 minutes, drain well. Cook 1 small, finely chopped onion with 1 chopped clove of garlic in 2 tablespoons olive oil until soft but not browned. Mix the onion with the rice. Add 1 tablespoon chopped fresh mint, salt and freshly ground black pepper, ½ teaspoon dried marjoram (or 2 teaspoons chopped fresh) and 4 peeled and chopped ripe tomatoes.

Blanch about 36 vine leaves in boiling water for 1 minute, drain and dry on absorbent kitchen paper. Place a heaped teaspoonful of the rice mixture on a vine leaf. Fold the leaf over the filling, then roll up into a neat parcel. Place in an ovenproof dish. Heat 300 ml/½ pint white wine, or half and half wine and stock, and gently pour this over the leaves. Cover tightly and cook in the oven at 180°C/ 350°F/gas 4 for about 1¼ hours, until most of the liquid has been absorbed. Drizzle a little olive oil over the leaves, cover and allow to cool completely, then chill overnight.

W

WEATHER

Forget it! Inexpensive waterproof canopies (from camping suppliers) solve most weather problems. A clean, open, well-ventilated garage is a good place to barbecue. Winter barbecues are fun. Make sure everyone knows and wear plenty of warm clothes. Offer mulled wine or cider and combine the food with a healthy walk before or after eating. Make everyone watch the barbecue even if you eat inside.

WHITING

Whiting is bland and the fillets are coarser and firmer than plaice. They barbecue reasonably well, given that you take care when turning them not to break the fish.

Quick Satay Whiting

Mix 2 teaspoons crunchy peanut butter, ½ teaspoon soy sauce, ½ teaspoon ground coriander, ½ chopped clove of garlic, 2 teaspoons oil and a little seasoning. Skin 4 small whiting fillets. Lay them skinned side down and spread the peanut mixture over the top. Fold the fillets in half and press each one firmly to sandwich the peanut mixture inside. Brush the outside with a little oil (try a mixture of corn oil with a few drops of sesame oil) and cook for 6–8 minutes, turning once, until the fish is lightly browned and cooked through.

WINE CUP

A refreshing, fruity punch. Thinly slice 1 lemon and cut the slices in half. Similarly, thinly slice an orange and quarter the slices. Mix the fruit with a few fine slices of cucumber and 100 g/4 oz hulled and halved strawberries. Add 150 ml/¼ pint brandy and a bottle of medium dry white wine. Cover and chill for 2 hours. Add ice cubes and 1.15 litres/2 pints soda water, sparkling mineral water or lemonade just before serving. The lemonade makes a sweet punch, the others a dry alternative. If you like, use part lemonade and part soda or mineral water, tasting the punch until it suits your palate. Makes about 20 glasses.

Y

YOGURT

Use it for marinating chicken, turkey or lamb before

cooking, adding herbs, spices and other flavourings.

Yogurt with Honey

Buy thick, creamy Greek yogurt, allowing one large carton for two portions. Have it well chilled in individual glass dishes. Just before serving, swirl some honey on top of the yogurt. Top each portion with roughly chopped, toasted blanched almonds.

Caramelized Yogurt Peaches

Place 4 fresh, ripe peaches in a bowl and pour over freshly boiling water. Leave for a few minutes, drain and peel. Halve the peaches and discard the stones, then thickly slice the fruit and place in a flameproof dish. Top with a thick layer of Greek yogurt (the amount will depend on the width of the dish but allow at least two large tubs) and a thick layer of soft brown sugar. Put under a hot grill for a few minutes, until the sugar melts and bubbles. Serve at once.

Yogurt Apple Cooler

Pour 600 ml/1 pint well chilled natural yogurt into a jug. Gradually stir in 600 ml/1 pint apple juice (select juice that is naturally fairly sweet) and top with sprigs of mint. Chill for 30 minutes. To make individual portions, half-fill a glass with yogurt and stir in an equal volume of apple juice. Add a sprig of mint and ice to serve.

RECIPE INDEX

THE FAMILY MATTERS SERIES